The Poems of Mao Tse-tung

Drawing by Willis Barnstone

The Poems
of Mao Tse-tung

Translation, Introduction, Notes by
WILLIS BARNSTONE

In Collaboration with
KO CHING-PO

HARPER & ROW, PUBLISHERS

New York, Evanston, San Francisco, London

THE POEMS OF MAO TSE-TUNG. English translation copyright © 1972 by Bantam Books, Inc. All rights reserved. Printed in the United States of America. No part of this book may be used or reproduced in any manner whatsoever without written permission except in the case of brief quotations embodied in critical articles and reviews. For information address Harper & Row, Publishers, Inc., 49 East 33rd Street, New York, N.Y. 10016. Published simultaneously in Canada by Fitzhenry & Whiteside Limited, Toronto.

FIRST EDITION

STANDARD BOOK NUMBER: 06–010219–5

LIBRARY OF CONGRESS CATALOG CARD NUMBER: 72–75623

for Robert Payne

who years ago when I was a student in
Paris spoke with enthusiasm about a
Chinese poet, Mao Tse-tung, when no
one else seemed to know or care

CONTENTS

ACKNOWLEDGMENTS

Many thanks are due to Professors Newton Stallknecht, Philip West, Robert and Brenda Schildgen, Harry Geduld, Philip Appleman, Ssu-yu, Alvin Rosenfeld, André Reszler, and Ulrich Weisstein for reading the texts and making helpful suggestions. My special thanks to Professor Liu Wu-chi of Indiana University, son of the poet Liu Ya-tzu, to whom Mao addresses two of his poems. Professor Liu offered much information about his father, Mao's poetry mentor, and about the special relationship of the two poets. I also wish to thank Mr. Christopher Janus, whose interest in China matches his concern for Greece, and Ms. Bonnie Crown of the Asia Society for her encouragement and good deeds.

I. Introduction

Poetry in China is the Great Wall. Or as more accurately represented in Chinese characters, the Long Wall.[1]* Its long uniform strength crosses the northern deserts, rides nimbly and evenly over Tu Fu's yellow hills, and winds through the great snow mountain ranges. It has held in civilization, at times walled it in, from the barbarian outer kingdoms; yet as Mao writes in the poem "Snow," from the Long Wall one sees, in both directions, the vastness of the natural world.

Like the Wall though even older, Chinese poetry stalks through nature and historical events. It is an even structure, traditional, with balanced formal patterns. However it rises or plunges or twists, it is quietly constant in its dimensions. It holds in Chinese civilization—from the time the first characters were inscribed on oracle bones and tortoise shells near the Hunan River. Wherever it goes, it is an eye that sees an image, in present time, the only tense in Chinese. The eye sees with candor and reveals only what it sees. A simple yet complex lens. For in this poetry of observation are many depths of focus and a complexity of allusions. It is the reader who sees beyond the clear picture. Mao's poems—moving through nature and historical events—follow the formal traditions of ancient Chinese song and of the magnificent Long Wall.

Mao's Life and the Revolution

"I was born in the village of Shao Shan, in . . . Hunan province, in 1893. My father was a poor peasant and while still young was

*Notes on the Introduction begin on page 26.

3

obliged to join the army because of heavy debts. He was a soldier for many years. Later on he returned to the village where I was born, and by saving carefully and gathering together a little money through small trading and other enterprise he managed to buy back his land."[2] So Mao began his biographical account to the American journalist Edgar Snow in July 1936, in Pao An, a desert region of northern Shensi where he was living in a cave, directing the Red enclave, and writing his essays on revolution and government.

"I began studying in a local primary school when I was eight and remained there until I was thirteen years old. In the early morning and at night I worked on the farm. During the day I read the Confucian *Analects* and the *Four Classics*."[3] Mao describes his father as severe and fearful. "He hated to see me idle, and if there were no books to be kept he put me to work at farm tasks. He was a hot-tempered man and frequently beat both me and my brothers. He gave us no money whatever, and the most meager food. On the fifteenth of every month he made a concession to his laborers and gave them eggs with their rice, but never meat. To me he gave neither eggs nor meat. My mother was a kind woman, generous and sympathetic, and ever ready to share what she had. She pitied the poor and often gave them rice when they came to ask for it during famines."[4] Mao speaks of rebellion against his father, of once threatening to leap into a pond and drown himself if the beatings did not stop, and of certain small gains he made in his family by refusing to be submissive.

"My father had had two years of schooling and he could read enough to keep books. My mother (a devout Buddhist) was wholly illiterate. Both were from peasant families. I was the family 'scholar.' I knew the Classics, but disliked them. What I enjoyed were the romances of Old China, and especially stories of rebellion."[5] Before he was ten he began his lifetime reading of the great Chinese novels: *The Dream of the Red Chamber*, *The Journey to the West* (translated by Arthur Waley as *Monkey*), *The Three*

Kingdoms, Water Margin (translated by Pearl Buck as *All Men Are Brothers*). Though later he mastered the earlier classics—he quotes from Confucius in his poems—at this age he disdained the five Chinese Classics. In part he was rebelling against his father, who was once defeated in a lawsuit because of an "apt Classical quotation used by his adversary in the Chinese court. . . . He wanted me to read something practical like the Classics, which could help him in winning lawsuits."[6]

As a child of peasants in a Hunan village, Mao had his roots in the land. He knew the people's life and their problems. Later he was to say, "Whoever wins the peasants will win China. . . . Whoever solves the land question will win the peasants."[7] And his intimacy with the land was also to provide him with the basic metaphor for his poetry. All is expressed through the presence of nature. A half century after his first departure from Shaoshan, Mao recalls in the poem "Return to Shaoshan" the "vague dream" of his childhood in Hunan, Land of the Hibiscus, and its orchards, serfs, warlords, and rice fields.

Mao was sent to another school, in nearby Hsiang Hsiang, when he was sixteen. Then in 1911 he went to the provincial capital of Changsha, where he was to remain until 1918, when he graduated from the First Normal School of Hunan. These were his "turbulent" student years. He was an omnivorous reader and inhabited the Hunan Provincial Library, where he remained reading, oblivious of people and food, from opening time in the morning until it closed at night. "I read many books, studied world geography and world history. There for the first time I saw and studied with great interest a map of the world. I read Adam Smith's *The Wealth of Nations*, and Darwin's *Origin of Species,* and a book on ethics by John Stuart Mill. I read the works of Rousseau, Spencer's *Logic*, and a book on law written by Montesquieu. I mixed poetry and romances, and the tales of ancient Greece, with serious study of history and geography of Russia, America, England, France, and other countries."[8] He was an ardent student of philosophy, reading intensively in the ancient Greeks, Spinoza, Kant, and Goethe. He was especially affected by F. Paulsen's *A System of Ethics*. Later he would discover Hegel and Marx.

But these were also years of political awakening, his first writing, his first lasting friendships. The excitement of the age is best conveyed in his poem "Changsha." For a brief period in 1911 he had also served six months in the republican army. China was in turmoil, in sporadic revolution by the armies of Sun Yat-sen against the Manchus and Yuan Shih-kai, who wished to restore the monarchy.

In these days of study and agitation Mao gathered groups of students around him. He founded the New Citizens Society in April 1918, a discussion group of young activists. Mao relates that they talked endlessly of the great issues; he and his companions also became energetic physical culturists. "In the winter holidays we tramped through the fields, up and down mountains, along city walls, and across the streams and rivers. If it rained we took off our shirts and called it a rain bath. When the sun was hot we also doffed shirts and called it a sun bath. In the spring we shouted that this was a new sport called 'wind bathing.' We slept in the open when frost was already falling and even in November swam in the cold rivers. All this went on under the title of 'body training.' Perhaps it helped much to build the physique which I was to need so badly later on in many marches back and forth across South China, and on the Long March from Kiangsi to the Northwest."[9]

At twenty-five, in 1918, Mao graduated from the Normal School in Changsha and went to Peking, the Forbidden City.[10] There he wanted to study at Peking National University, to bury himself in its library, and also to join in the life of this city which, with its huge student movements, was beginning to change the political life of the country. Through the intervention of an acquaintance, Li Tao-chao, a professor of political economy, he obtained a menial position in the newspaper room of the university library. "My position was so low that people avoided me," he wrote.[11] "I knew then," he said, "that there was something wrong. For hundreds of years the scholars had moved away from the people, and I began to dream of a time when the scholars would teach the coolies, for surely the coolies deserve teaching as much as the rest."[12]

In Peking he immersed himself in poetry, especially that of the Tang dynasty poet Tsen Tsan (722?–770?), who wrote of winter expeditions against the Huns who roamed on horseback between the Dagger River and the Hill of Gold Mountains. Later Mao borrowed freely from Tsen's depiction of early Han campaigns across China. Mao read the Russians as well, Tolstoy and the anarchists Kropotkin and Bakunin. For a period of some six months he announced to his friends that he was an anarchist. He also fell in love with Yang Kai-hui, daughter of a professor of philosophy, whom he married three years later. (See his poem "The Gods.") Mao describes this colorful period:

My own living conditions in Peking were quite miserable, and in contrast the beauty of the old capital was a vivid and living compensation. I stayed in a place called San Yen-ching [Three-Eyes Well], in a little room which held seven other people. When we were all packed fast on the *kang* [a large bed made of earth heated from underneath] there was scarcely room enough for any of us to breathe. I used to have to warn people on each side of me when I wanted to turn over. But in the parks and the old palace grounds I saw the early northern spring, I saw the white plum blossoms flower while the ice still held solid over Pei Hai with the ice crystals hanging from them and remembered the description of the scene by the Tang poet Tsen Tsan, who wrote about Pei Hai's winter-jeweled trees looking "like ten thousand peach trees blossoming." The innumerable trees of Peking aroused my wonder and admiration.[13]

When Mao returned to Changsha in March 1919 he took a more direct role in politics. He became editor of the *Hsiang River Review*, wrote essays, organized discussion groups. He was also teaching in the Hsiu-yeh Primary School. By the time of the May

4 student uprising in Peking, which shook the national government, he had begun to read Marx and think of himself as a Marxist. He went again to Peking to represent the New Citizens Society and to protest against the actions of the Hunan governor Chang Ching-yao, who had suppressed his periodical and other nationalist publications. In April 1920 we find him in Shanghai. He had sold his fur coat for the fare; he wrote to the headmaster of his primary school: "I am working as a laundryman. The difficult part of my job is not washing but delivery, as most of my earnings from washing have to be spent on tram tickets which are so expensive."[14] This was Mao's first experience as a city worker.

Mao continued to read, and to wander about the countryside, visiting shrines and organizing groups in the cities. In late June or early July of 1921 he was one of twelve members who attended the First Congress of the Chinese Communist Party, which met in Shanghai. Although the party had vague beginnings a few years earlier with the existence of Marxist study groups, this was the effective start of organized communism in China.

The main revolutionary group in China at this time, however, was not the Chinese Communist Party (CCP) but the Kuomintang (KMT) under Dr. Sun Yat-sen. It was his armies that had fought against the Manchus and established the republic. The KMT (People's party) was then a loose political grouping of left- and right-wing forces, dominated initially by the left, with strong backing from the Soviet Union. Mao joined the KMT and was a delegate at its First Congress in 1924. He was elected an alternate member of the Central Executive Committee, and became head of the Kuomintang Propaganda Bureau and editor of its publication, *Political Weekly*. At this time of the first "United Front," there was no contradiction in being a member of both the Communist Party and the Kuomintang and it was indeed his position as a Kuomintang official that gave him his first national political experience and prominence.

During this period he met Chiang Kai-shek, who had just returned from the Soviet Union, glowing with accounts of Russian industrialization. The young austere KMT officer, with his golden earrings and an imposing bearing, had been sent to Moscow in 1923 by Sun Yat-sen for military and political instruction. The Russians were always to hold the aristocratic general in special esteem. When Chiang was arrested in 1936 by one of his commanders, the "Young Marshal" Chang Hsueh-liang, it was the Russian envoy, André Malraux suggests, who intervened to prevent his execution.[15] Malraux also records Mao's words on Chiang: "The Russians' feelings were for Chiang Kai-shek. When he escaped from China, the Soviet ambassador was the last person to wish him goodbye."[16]

The entente between the CCP and the KMT was nevertheless precarious. Mao worked avidly in both groups, in Shanghai, Canton, Hunan. He organized a miners' strike and actively worked to organize peasant unions. His hope lay with the peasants, whom he saw as the basis of revolutionary change in China, and in 1926 he wrote his well-known "Report on an Investigation into the Peasant Movement in Hunan." In this he was directly rejecting Marxist and Russian theory, which saw the urban proletariat as the basis of political activity.

Meanwhile events were moving quickly in the new China. Opposing forces of the left and right within the KMT organized and formed armies. In 1925 Sun Yat-sen died of cancer. A year later Chiang Kai-shek attempted a coup d'etat in Canton and failed. Then, on April 12, 1927, he made a second coup in Shanghai, succeeded, and effectively took over the KMT. He ordered the "complete extermination of the Communists and Socialists in the city," the so-called white massacre of thousands of workers and CCP members, which was followed in May by the massacre in Hunan.[17] In July the KMT ordered the arrest of Mao, who was by now organizing peasant associations into military units. The entente was broken, and while there were to be later truces between KMT and CCP forces, induced by the Japanese invasion, the civil war had indeed begun, and was to endure for twenty-two years.

The flame was lit. The peasants in Hunan province rebelled. The landlords struck back, and there were executions and terror on both sides. The KMT armies were marching and the "white terror" was launched throughout the Yangtze Valley. Chou En-lai barely escaped when some four hundred party members were executed in Shanghai. In July, Chou organized an armed uprising in the capital city of Nanking. It failed. With the CCP proscribed by government order, Mao was declared a "red bandit." He in turn, with great speed, began to group peasant unions and Hanyang miners into the First Workers' and Peasants' Revolutionary Army. By September 1927 he was ready and launched what became known as the Autumn Harvest Uprising in Hunan and Kiangsi provinces. Some small cities were briefly captured, but support did not come from Changsha and this uprising also failed. Mao himself was taken prisoner while traveling between worker and peasant groups. He writes:

I was captured by some *min-t'uan* [militia], working with the Kuomintang. The Kuomintang terror was then at its height and hundreds of suspected Reds were being shot. I was ordered to be taken to the *min-t'uan* headquarters, where I was to be killed. Borrowing several tens of dollars from a comrade, however, I attempted to bribe the escort to free me. The ordinary soldiers were mercenaries, with no special interest in seeing me killed, and they agreed to release me, but the subaltern in charge refused to permit it. I therefore decided to attempt to escape, but had no opportunity to do so until I was within about two hundred yards of the *min-t'uan* headquarters. At that point I broke loose and ran into the fields.

I reached a high place, above a pond, with some tall grass surrounding it and there I hid until sunset. The soldiers pursued me, and forced some peasants to help them search. Many times they came very near, once or twice so close that I could almost have touched them, but somehow I escaped discovery, although half a dozen times I gave up hope, feeling certain I would be recaptured. At last, when it was dusk, they abandoned the search. At once I set off across the mountains, traveling all night. I had no shoes and my feet were badly bruised. On the road I met a peasant who befriended me, gave me shelter and later guided me to the next district. I had seven dollars with me, and used this to buy some shoes, an umbrella, and food. When at last I reached the peasant guards safely, I had only two coppers in my pocket.[18]

After this Mao gathered together the remnants of four regiments, about one thousand men, and in October led them to establish the first Communist base in the high mountain area called Chingkangshan, in Kiangsi province. (See his poem "Chingkang Mountain.") There the future Red Army was formed and there Mao wrote his three rules and six injunctions by which guerrilla warfare was to be fought.[19] On this great mountain of pine and bamboo, desolately cold in the winter, the army grew. Volunteers swelled it to more than eleven thousand by January 1928. Mao was joined on Chingkangshan by Chu Teh, who was to be the other main military leader of the Red Army and Mao's most trusted companion. Although they had few weapons, no radio, and limited food supplies, they began to fight skirmishes in the Kiangsi hills. Soon they were fifty thousand. The Kuomintang reacted with its Five Annihilation Campaigns, the first of which, in late December 1930, ended in a disastrous defeat of the KMT army and the capture of extensive military supplies. (See the poems "First Siege" and "Second Siege.")

In the next years the Kuomintang carried out its Second, Third, and Fourth Annihilation Campaigns, each with more massive armies against increasingly large Red forces. The KMT failed in its objectives. Finally, in 1933, with the aid of his military adviser, General von Falkenhausen, Chiang introduced a new strategy: to surround the Red Army in Kiangsi and Fukien provinces with a ring of blockhouses, "a new Wall of China hemming it in."[20] By the next year the KMT armies of nearly a million men, with tanks and four hundred planes, inflicted severe losses on the Red Army, which in October 1934 found itself trapped. Of this period Mao wrote: "It was a serious mistake to meet the vastly superior Nanking forces in positional warfare, at which the Red Army was neither technically nor spiritually at its best."[21] He expressed it more bluntly when he said: "We panicked, and we fought stupidly."[22] On October 16, 1934, with the Kuomintang about to launch a new powerful offensive, Mao decided to break through the encirclement. With some eighty-five thousand men he set out from Yatu in southern Kiangsi on the epic Long March.

The March began as a retreat, an escape from a cage. Its vague objective was Shensi in northwest China, where it could join a soviet[23] that was safe from KMT attack and could also serve as a base from which to fight the Japanese. The army wandered over much of China, reaching Tibet in the southwest, crossing desert, Tartar steppes, the immense Great Snow Mountain, Ma An-shan, and the terrible Grasslands. At the beginning they traveled mainly by night in bad weather—which aided them in escaping attack from KMT planes. In the first month the army fought nine major battles and broke through four lines of blockhouses and many regiments, but it lost a third of its men. Mao himself was ill with fever during the first months, yet he traveled most of the time on foot. He carried on his back his famous knapsack, divided into nine compartments from which he directed Red China: maps, books, paper, documents, and a few more items. "He possessed a sun-helmet, a torn umbrella, two uniforms, one cotton sheet, two blankets, a lantern, a water-jug, a special bowl to hold cakes of three layer rice, and a silver-grey woollen sweater."[24] Even then, whenever the army camped he continued his practice of working late into the night, studying maps, reading and rereading the classical novels he carried with him, and writing poems. This year of extreme physical hardships and ventures was perhaps his most prolific year as a poet. Nature's harshness tested him— *"L'homme se découvre quand il se mesure avec l'obstacle,"* Saint-Exupéry wrote. There is no complaint in the poems; rather, the pleasure of his intimacy with nature, its severity, enormity, and beauty.

12

The most famous episode of the March was the crossing of the bridge over the Tatu River. The old iron bridge had had most of its wooden planks removed by KMT soldiers on the other side. Some twenty-four volunteers began to cross over, dangling from the chains and swinging across link by link. They were picked off one by one and fell into the roaring gorge three hundred feet below. But some reached the last planks on the other side, which had been set on fire, overwhelmed the surprised enemy, and secured the bridge.

After Tatu, the army turned north. In the snow mountains Mao found comparative safety, yet the prodigious heights weakened his army. Many perished and pack animals and supplies were abandoned en masse. It was the swamps of the Grasslands, however, that were remembered with horror. Near Tibet his men had been attacked by seemingly invisible Mantzu tribesmen. Now they were passing again through a region of hostile tribes. No food was available. Robert Payne writes: "They dug up what seemed to be turnips, but these proved to be poisonous. The water made them ill. The winds buffeted them, hailstorms were followed by snow. Ropes were laid down to guide them across the marshlands, but the ropes vanished in the quicksands. They lost their few remaining pack animals. A small column would be seen walking across a sea of thick, damp, foggy grasses, and then the whole column would disappear."[25]

The army was near the end of its march. They had passed through provinces populated by many millions of people, and when they were not fighting or simply surviving, they engaged in political proselytizing: mass meetings, pamphlets, even theater performances. They redistributed land and attempted to win over the peasants. Malraux records the last days of the venture: "On October 20, 1935, at the foot of the Great Wall, Mao's horsemen, wearing hats of leaves and mounted on little shaggy ponies like those of prehistoric cave paintings, joined up with the three communist armies of Shensi, of which Mao took command. He had twenty thousand men left, of whom seven thousand had been with him all the way from the south. They had covered six and a half thousand miles. Almost all the women had died, and the children had been left along the way. The Long March was at an end."[26] (See Mao's poem "The Long March.")

Shensi is a region of desert and loess hills in north China, an area relatively safe from attack, where the Red forces consolidated and increased their strength. When there was drought and famine, Mao sent the troops out to work on the farms with the peasants. Mao himself always lived and dressed plainly. In Pao An he worked and slept in a cave outside the city. Often working without sleep for many nights in a row, there in Yenan he wrote his five best-known extended essays: *On a Prolonged War, The New Democracy, The Strategic Problems of China's Revolutionary Wars, The Chinese Revolution and the Communist Party of China*, and *Coalition Government*.

The Red and KMT forces continued to skirmish. Then suddenly on December 12, 1936, the "Young Marshal" Chang Hsueh-liang, in command of a large army of Tungpei forces, arrested Chiang Kai-shek. He contacted Mao, and Chou En-lai flew to Sian as Mao's delegate. Mao did not want the Generalissimo's life taken. It would signal the impending Japanese forces to stream across the Manchurian border. By spring an accord was reached, the so-called Second United Front, the basic agreement being that PLA (People's Liberation Army) and KMT forces were not to attack each other, and would unite against the Japanese. On July 15, 1937, the Japanese attacked the Marco Polo bridge and invaded China.

During the long years that followed, despite their agreement, there continued to be small-scale struggles between PLA and KMT armies. Chiang retreated to Chungking and avoided major clashes with the Japanese, hoping to conserve his military strength. Instead, through inaction and inefficiency, the KMT army grew weaker, unwieldy, and dispirited. But Mao fought the Japanese almost continuously and in doing so developed his guerrilla armies for the later civil war. It was the Japanese who prepared the way for Chinese communism, much as Nazi Germany had done for Soviet communism in Eastern Europe.

After the Japanese surrender in August 1945, there was a pause. The power vacuum could be filled in many ways. The Russians were in Manchuria and Stalin counseled his Chinese comrades to dissolve their army, seek a modus vivendi with Chiang, and join in a coalition government.[27] Meanwhile the United States sent Ambassador P. J. Hurley to Yenan and Chungking, and he persuaded Mao to come to Chungking and meet with Chiang for the purpose of ending all hostilities in China. Under an American safe-conduct shield, Mao came to Chungking, August 28, 1945. It was on this plane trip, he told Robert Payne in Yenan a year later, that he wrote "Snow," which was to become his best-known poem.

"I wrote it in the airplane. It was the first time I had ever been in an airplane. I was astonished by the beauty of my country from the air—and there were other things."

"What other things?"

"So many. You must remember when the poem was written. It was when there was so much hope in the air, when we trusted the Generalissimo." A moment later he said: "My poems are so stupid—you mustn't take them seriously."[28]

Mao spent a month and a half in Chungking. There were polite exchanges, telegrams of goodwill, and even parties and toasts. The evening before Mao left, while the two leaders were at the opera together, one of Mao's aides was shot and killed in Mao's car waiting outside the theater. Yet while negotiations were taking place and Chou En-lai did sign an agreement not to renew the civil war, it was immediately clear that the paper meant nothing. Chiang attacked in Manchuria, Kiangsu, and Anhuei. Then in 1946 President Truman sent General George Marshall as his personal envoy to China with the aim of unifying the country and averting large-scale civil war. With Marshall's authority and prestige there was again genuine hope in all quarters for a peaceful and democratic solution. His mission had some initial success. Chiang and Mao ordered a cease-fire on January 10, 1946. But on Marshall's departure, clashes began again. The American general returned, aided by the new American ambassador, Dr. J. Leighton Stuart, who proposed a committee of five to govern China, with representation from both sides. Chiang rejected the Stuart plan. Thereafter there were no serious attempts at mediation. Reluctantly and with much bitterness and recriminations from all sides, America resumed its lend-lease military aid to the KMT. Fierce battles ensued and as America poured in supplies to demoralized and poorly led KMT armies, the matériel was sold or surrendered almost immediately to the Red forces.[29] Provincial capitals began to fall. The civil war which Mao had thought would last at least several years longer was coming to an end. In late January 1949 Peking was captured by Communist troops. Nanking fell in April, Hangchow and Shanghai in May. On October 1, 1949, Mao Tse-tung, accompanied by Chu Teh and Chou En-lai, stood before immense crowds on a balcony of the "Gate of Heavenly Peace," the palace from which emperors had ruled China, the Middle Kingdom. There in his drab cloth cap and plain clothes, he proclaimed the foundation of the People's Republic of China. A new dynasty was officially brought into being.

About the Poems

In Chinese poetry the image is always clear. When Mao or a classical poet looks at nature, he is often content to let nature have its own being, to be self-contained, to have its own beauty and not be man's mirror or depend on an intrusion of man for its value. To call this pantheism is misleading, for such general terms impose an ideology on the poet, and we are interested here in the poet's eye, not his spiritual doctrine. In the poem—like the characters in which they are written—everything or almost everything is visual. And this is true whether the poet resorts to history, myth, personal memory, or immediate passion. Clarity is the jade virtue. Even in a night poem or in a passage of bitterness or pessimism, a clarity illumines thought, feeling, or object.

Writing poems is perhaps a more natural and common act in the East than in the West. The Western postromantic poet is popularly thought to be a race apart and the George Seferis, Wallace Stevens, or William Carlos Williams—diplomat, insurance executive, or doctor—inevitably surprises us. It is expected, however, that the Japanese emperor be also a poet—as were most Chinese emperors—and it was natural for Tojo to write poems in his cell the night before his execution. Prior to the republic in China, it had been for centuries obligatory for all civil servants to demonstrate, by examination, their ability to produce a poem. At one level the writing of verse has been a "filling in" of traditional song patterns, a proof of literacy.

It need not surprise us then that the leader of a quarter of mankind, of more people than any leader in the history of the world, the Old Man of the Mountains as Malraux calls him, is a poet. What is unexpected, however, is that he is a major poet, an original master. In his peculiar way, he has offered few poems for publication, although he has written all his life.[30] Mao has written poems obsessively, during years of wandering and living in caves, writing all night, evening after evening, and then throwing away his "scribbles."[31] He knows there are things more important than poetry, and this attitude contributes paradoxically to the relentless power and authenticity of the poems. It is in part his genuine if perverse modesty that informs the poems with special value. He was sixty-five before publishing his first collection. God and the state do special things to the self-image of their poets.

Formally Mao uses two classical patterns of Chinese song, the *tzu* and the *lu*. (See Chinese Versification, page 142.) He is considered a traditional poet. He writes in the "old style," he confesses, although here too his self-disparagement should not distract us from his freshness of vision. In a letter to a friend, Tsang Keh-chia, who had asked him to prepare some poems for publication in a new magazine, he characterizes his poems:

January 12, 1957

DEAR KEH-CHIA AND OTHER COMRADES,

I received your kind letter some time ago and am sorry to be so late in replying. As you wished, I have now copied out on separate sheets all my poems in the old style that I can remember as well as the eight that you sent me. They make eighteen altogether. Herewith I enclose these poems and put them at your disposal.

Up to now I have never wanted to make these things known in any formal way, because they are in the old style and I was afraid this might encourage a wrong trend and exercise a bad influence on your people. Besides, they are not much as poetry, and there is nothing outstanding about them. However, if you think that they should be published and thus misprints can be also corrected in those poems already in circulation, you may do what you please with them.

It is very good that we are to have the magazine *Poetry*. I hope it will grow and flourish exceedingly. Of course our poetry should be written mainly in the modern form. We may write some verse in classical forms as well, but it would not be advisable to encourage young people to do this, because these forms would cramp their thought and are also difficult to master. I merely put forward this opinion for your consideration.

Fraternal greetings!

MAO TSE-TUNG[32]

Following the rules of Chinese versification, Mao fills in some twenty-five classical forms. He borrows or alludes to many lines of Tang (618–907) and Sung (960–1127) poets, and contains nature behind a Long Wall of set tonal patterns, rhyme, and line lengths. The structured form keeps together the images of his inventive eye. For Mao leaps from image to image. With a Pindaric sweep he moves elliptically and mythically from place to place, century to century. As he walks across the Middle Kingdom he records its modern history, which he is living and creating, and uses the historical and mythical past to illuminate the present.

> White clouds hang over the Mountain of Nine Questions.
> The daughters of the emperor rode the wind
> > down to a jade meadow
> where a thousand tears fell and dappled the bamboo.
> > > > "To a Friend"

In the early poems Mao depicts the first battles of the peasant army. There is a sequence of events, and the poems are connected like lyrical fragments of a larger epic. As in Pindar's athletic odes, there is nothing tragic in the war poems; rather an enthusiasm, even amid suffering, and an enjoyment of victory after the contest. Victory may be climbing a mountain, sweeping away the god of disease, surviving the Long March. Nature is beautiful and severe; yet its harshness is benevolent, for it tests and forms the author and his companions. In many of the exultant poems of the Long March one finds the same manly intimacy with snow mountains or friends as in the epic of the *Cid*, where Rodrigo, a leader in exile, crosses the steppes and rivers of Spain, seeking and physically enjoying the ethical pursuit of national unification amid civil war and invasion from the outside.

> Our soldiers point and look eagerly
> > south to Kwangtung,
> onion green and sensual in the distance.
> > > > "Huichang"

> The far snows of Minshan only make us happy
> and when the army pushes through, we all laugh.
> > > > "The Long March"

While these lines deal with national events, they do not have the weakness of much public poetry, in which the experience is gained secondhand. Later changes in mainland China made these first military encounters historically important. At the time, however, they were not quantitative or political abstractions but Mao's personal engagement with history. He invokes a particular power in the way his words are heard as both a collective and a single voice.

> Do you remember
> how in the middle of the river
> we hit the water, splashed, and how our waves
>   slowed down the swift junks?
>
> "Changsha"

These last passages require a brief discussion of literature and politics. The sharp division between social and personal poetry is recent. Before the middle of the nineteenth century the poet did not necessarily have to choose between public and private worlds. Archilochos and Dante, Blake and Shelley were at home in both worlds. By the end of the nineteenth century, however, Arthur Symons was warning us that "the poet has no more part in society than a monk in domestic life."[33] Although many years have passed, we are still uneasy about the conjunction of public streets and private souls. But we are moving nevertheless toward the poets like Yeats and Lowell and Voznesensky, who speak for nation and for self, who connect rather than dissociate the two identities.

Historical or political events hover around many of Mao's poems. The climate is revolution, an army wandering out against the elements, a frequent theme in classical Chinese poetry. The relation of politics to literature is often similar to that of religion to literature; the strength of religious or political conviction can both provoke a poet's artistry and make his poem authentic. We may share or fully reject the history or metaphysics that led to the poem; but if the poem is successful, the work of a consummate artist, we may be led into the poetic experience and momentarily find ourselves to be Maoists, Catholics, mystics, Achaeans—and intensely so.

The great mystical poet Saint John of The Cross eschews theological language. Similarly when Mao expresses happiness upon reading that the parasitic leech the schistosome has been eradicated in a section of southern China, he employs the most subtle images to convey the period of affliction and uses the Chinese mythical figure of the "cowherd who lives on a star" to celebrate the extirpation of the disease. The newspaper language in which he read the report has disappeared with the leech:

> Mauve waters and green mountains are nothing
> when the great ancient doctor Hua To could not defeat
> a tiny worm.
> A thousand villages collapsed, were choked with weeds,
> men were lost arrows.
> Ghosts sang in the doorway of a few desolate houses.
> "Saying Good-bye to the God of Disease" (1)

Never once does he descend to propaganda. Like the Spanish mystic Saint John of The Cross and Machado in his civil war poems, Mao uses only the concrete images of poetry to give us the history of modern China.

After 1949 the two decades of odyssey are over and the poems are more meditative. In the poem "Kunlun Mountain," written in the midst of the Long March, Mao dreamed of a time of peace in Europe, America, and China. Now that peace has come to China, he remembers childhood, and friends who have died, and he celebrates what he sees about him, again through nature and myth. He had written the poem "Snow" in 1945 for a friend, the older poet Liu Ya-tzu. Then, after the revolution triumphed, he exchanged two new poems with Liu, who had remained outside the Communist party, asking him to stay in Peking and join in the national reconstruction. Liu had said that he planned to return to his home in the south. Mao first recalls in two brief lines, poignant with nostalgia:

> I cannot forget how in Canton we drank tea
> and in Chungking went over our poems
>   when leaves were yellowing.

Then in asking Liu to consider remaining in Peking, he alludes to the Later Han dynasty poet Yen Kuang, who preferred to leave the court and become a fisherman in the Fuchun River. Mao writes gently that the waters of Kumming Lake (near the Imperial Palace in Peking) are not too shallow, and the two friends can watch fish together just as well there as in Liu's homeland:

> Don't say that waters of Kumming Lake are too shallow.
> We can watch fish better here than in the Fuchun
>   River in the south.
>   "Poem for Liu Ya-tzu" (1949)

In another poem a few years later, Mao addresses a woman friend, Li Shu-yi, whose husband had been killed in a battle against the Kuomintang in 1933. He couples the husband's death with that of his own wife, Yang Kai-hui, who was beheaded in 1930 by the warlord General Ho Chien. "The Gods" is a poem of astonishing tenderness, dreaminess, and joy. It is direct in its emotional appeal, yet each verse evokes the astronomy of ancient myth.

> I lost my proud poplar and you your willow.
> As poplar and willow they soar straight up
>   into the ninth heaven
> and ask the prisoner of the moon, Wu Kang, what is there.
> He offers them wine from the cassia tree.
>
> The lonely lady on the moon, Chang O,
>   spreads her vast sleeves
> and dances for these good souls in the unending sky.

Down on earth a sudden report of the tiger's defeat.
Tears fly down from a great upturned bowl of rain.

"The Gods"

In the note on this poem (page 132) I have tried to explain some
of the specific allusions. In his book *Poetry and Politics* the late
classicist C. M. Bowra goes into some detail about the particular
myth, which I quote here because it is relevant to some final
remarks about Mao's poetics. Bowra writes:

Behind this lies an ancient myth. Wu Kang, who had sought immortality,
was condemned by the gods to cut down the cassia-tree in the moon,
but every time he fells it, it becomes whole again. Mao imagines that his
own wife and his friend's husband are transported to the moon, where
Wu Kang, freed at last from his toil, welcomes them. The goddess in the
moon spreads her robes for a dance, and, on hearing of the defeat of the
Tiger, of hostile forces on earth, all burst into tears of joy. The whole
scheme fits together, and even the image of the Tiger is apt, since it too
comes from legend and is easily given a new application. The special
interest of Mao's myth is that he does not believe in it, but uses it to
convey the undying glory which his own wife and his friend's husband
have won. Mao, as we might expect, sometimes writes about public
events in a perfectly straightforward manner and feels no qualms about
it, but here he has chosen a myth because it exalts his subject and
underlines elements which mean a lot to him. Its imagery is rich in
associations, and the theme of dying for a cause is ennobled by them.[34]

We have seen that in Mao's few statements on his own poems,
he modestly dismisses them as being of little value. The main
published essays on Mao's poems in Peking and elsewhere are not
much help in evaluating and understanding them; except in offer-
ing useful annotation on allusions, studies of the poems tend to be
so full of admiration that there is much paean singing, little criti-
cism. Mao himself has written numerous essays on art and literature. While his comments on literature may have affected and
reflected recent writing in China, he follows little or none of his

own counsel. As he declared in his letter to Tsang Keh-chia, his poems are in the old style and he does not recommend them to the young, who must find their own way.

We read what Mao says, for example, about myth in his essay "Myth and Reality."[35] First he quotes Marx: "All mythology masters and dominates and shapes the forces of nature in and through the imagination, hence it disappears as soon as man gains mastery over the forces of nature." Mao continues:

Although stories of endless metamorphoses in mythology or nursery tales can delight people because they imaginatively embody man's conquest of the forces of nature and, moreover, the best mythology possesses, as Marx put it, "eternal charm," yet mythology is not based on the specific conditions of actual contradictions and therefore does not scientifically reflect reality. That is to say, in mythology or nursery tales the aspects that constitute contradiction have only a fancied identity, not a real one.

Yet as a traditional Chinese poet, Mao is a servant of Chinese mythology: not a poem is without its mythical allusion.

China of the future will always mark its history by the actions of the Hunanese leader who after twenty-two years of revolution radically changed the life of the nation. Mao's role in history, however, must not blind us to the original power and beauty of the poems, each line possessing natural authority and ease, strong and clear as his images of snow wastelands and greenblue mountains.

The lines flash synchronically with early Han expeditions and banners of the Long March, with a sacred yellow crane over an ancient Taoist hillside. It is a poetry of wandering armies, of heavens that freeze, convulse, or pause peacefully below the white cock of the sun-moon dawn. The tone is at once lyric and epic. The poems he has given us are without grief or despair; physical suffering is a test, not an end. Yet for all the complexity of time, myth, and historical allusion, Mao, like few good poets in our century, seems immediately accessible, indeed an easy poet—if

24

deceptively so. In this apparent simplicity, he has, like Robert Frost, that rare ability to speak to us on several levels at once. In the soundless calligraphy of Chinese ideograms, lucidly arranged, he records his vision of nature and man. Old and new China come together in his fresh poems in the traditional style.

NOTES ON THE INTRODUCTION

1. The Great Wall of China was begun by the first emperor of China, Shih Huang (247/6–210 B.C.), although there were even older walls and these were connected as part of his new structure. The earliest walls disappear into an earlier time, into the haze when history and poetry were first recorded. Shih Huang united the Six Kingdoms of China, abolished the feudal system, built many public works, and it is from his dynasty, the Chin (221–207 B.C.), that we derive the name China. (The Chinese words for the nation are *Chung Kuo,* meaning "Middle Kingdom," a Han dynasty name.) But while the first emperor built and united, he also systematically gathered and burned earlier books. So the age is also called the Period of the Great Destruction. The emperor wished time and history to begin with him. Ties between the Wall, books, and time are related by Jorge Luis Borges in his legendary "The Wall and the Books." Borges connects Shih Huang's new wall and his destruction of earlier writing with a preoccupation for controlling time—a reappearing theme in Borges, in Chinese poetry, and in Mao, a poet of recollection and anticipation.

For a full description of the actual building of the Wall by a Chinese worker and of its ultimate meaning, see Franz Kafka's "The Great Wall of China." Kafka proves that the Wall is so vast, so far from the emperor's palace in Peking, that no man can comprehend the whole empire; thus while the Wall will last for thousands of years, its vast expanse obliterates emperor, empire, and present time.

2. Edgar Snow, *Red Star over China,* 1st rev. ed. (New York: Grove Press, 1968), p. 130.

3. Ibid., p. 131. Snow's report here may be misleading; the *Analects* are normally considered one of the *Four Classics.*

4. Ibid., p. 132.

5. Ibid., p. 133.

6. Ibid., p. 134.

7. Edgar Snow, "Why China Went Red," in Emil Schulthess, *China* (New York: Viking Press, 1966), unpaged.

8. Snow, *Red Star over China*, p. 144.

9. Ibid., p. 147.

10. The Forbidden City is actually the imperial center of Peking, surrounded by the outer Tartar city, and this in turn by greater Peking. As used here, the term follows common usage as another name for the city of Peking and not only its old imperial center.

11. Jerome Ch'ên, *Mao and the Chinese Revolution* (London: Oxford University Press, 1965), p. 53.

12. Robert Payne, *Portrait of a Revolutionary: Mao Tse-tung* (New York: Abelard-Schuman, 1961), p. 58.

13. Snow, *Red Star over China*, p. 152.

14. Ch'ên, op. cit., p. 66.

15. André Malraux, *Anti-Memoirs*, trans. Terence Kilmartin (New York: Holt, Rinehart & Winston, 1968), p. 349.

16. Ibid., p. 363. Some scholars question the accuracy of Malraux's reporting.

17. Payne, op. cit., p. 102.

18. Snow, op. cit., pp. 165–66.

19. Originally there were six injunctions. These were later condensed and two more were added. The three rules and eight injunctions are:

    1. Obey orders at all times.

    2. Do not take even a needle or a piece of thread from the people.

    3. Turn in all confiscated property to headquarters.

and:

    1. Replace all doors when you leave a house and return the straw matting.

    2. Be courteous to the people, and help them when you can.

    3. Return all borrowed articles and replace all damaged goods.

    4. Be honest in all transactions with the peasants.

    5. Be sanitary–dig latrines at a safe distance from homes and fill them up with earth before leaving.

    6. Don't damage crops.

7. Don't molest women.

8. Never ill-treat prisoners of war.

(Payne, op. cit., p. 107.)

20. Malraux, op. cit., p. 327.

21. Snow, *Red Star over China*, p. 180.

22. Payne, op. cit., p. 144.

23. A soviet: Red territory in which a collective, economically self-sustaining state was established, controlled by the CCP and its armies. The first Chinese soviet was organized at Hailofeng in 1927.

24. Payne, op. cit., p. 147.

25. Ibid., p. 162.

26. Malraux, op. cit., p. 332.

27. Ch'ên, op. cit., p. 263.

28. Payne, op. cit., p. 225.

29. In order to present material as objectively as possible, remarks that might appear as politically partisan have been avoided. It is necessary to say, however, that the Kuomintang Army and Chiang's efforts to defeat the Red Army collapsed from within. From American and other reports, the consensus holds that the KMT government and army were inefficient, its leaders frequently corrupt. Its soldiers served unwillingly and deserted when they could. American lend-lease matériel was often sold outright for personal gain to the People's Liberation Army. People in territories liberated from the Japanese by the KMT were often in no better conditions than before, for the KMT government handled the economy ruinously. Inflation went uncurbed until the cost of printing banknotes caught up with their face value. Warlord rule was restored in the provinces and the peasants were alienated. By contrast, U.S. Ambassador J. Leighton Stuart wrote about the PLA: "In painful contrast [to the KMT] the Communist Party was free from private graft, officers and men lived very much together, simply and identically. . . . There was almost no maltreatment of the populace. They borrowed extensively but generally returned these articles or made restitutions." (*Fifty Years in China* [New York: Random House, 1954], p. 242.) See Note 19 on the rules and injunctions of the PLA.

30. Mao did not publish a collection of poems until nineteen appeared in two numbers of the Chinese periodical *Poetry* in 1957 and January 1958. He was then sixty-five years old. During the years in Yenan he

printed for a few friends a collection of some seventy poems under the title *Wind Sand Poems*, including a long poem called "Grass," dealing with the march through the Grasslands. This book has not been reprinted publicly.

31. In "The Poetry of Mao Tse-tung," which appeared in the *Literary Review*, vol. 2, no. 1 (Autumn 1958), Payne speaks of retrieving two of Mao's poems from a pair of lieutenants who remembered them. He describes the scene (p. 78): "They said he was always writing poems during boring party meetings, and when he had finished, he would simply toss them on the floor. Usually they were picked up, but they were treasured less for the poetry—few of his lieutenants had any interest in verse—than as examples of calligraphy, which curiously resembled the man: very pale and soft in speech, with the air of a scholar and a dreamer. No one looking at his poems or his calligraphy would suspect the terrifying strength behind the silken mask."

32. Mao Tse-tung, *On Art and Literature*, trans. People's Literature Publishing House, Peking (Peking: Foreign Language Press, 1960), pp. 137–38.

33. In an essay on Yeats and public poetry, Archibald MacLeish quotes Symons. In the same volume MacLeish has several chapters on private and public vision. (*Poetry and Experience* [Baltimore: Penguin Books, 1964], p. 113.) Bowra (see next note) and MacLeish have written extensively about the division between public themes and private vision. Both argue that only since the mid-nineteenth century have most poets felt the need to choose between personal and public worlds. It would be reductive to suggest that up to a given period no such conflict existed and that suddenly an absolute split appeared. Today, however, we are more aware of divisions between the poet who withdraws from society and the poet in a political context, and we have developed a vocabulary to distinguish between the schools—classifications not used in the past for Horace or Dante or Shakespeare, who clearly operated, without conflict, in both worlds. So we speak of confessional and committed poets, of hermetic and engagé writers, of bourgeois narcissists and Marxist social realists. Spanish poetry, for example, has been divided for thirty years into opposing schools of *poesía social* and *poesía existencial* (social versus existential poetry). An instance of extreme awareness of such division may be found in Alan Bold's informative and polemical introduc-

tion to the recent *Penguin Book of Socialist Verse* (Harmondsworth: 1970), pp. 33–58.

34. C. M. Bowra, *Poetry and Politics 1900–1960* (Cambridge: Cambridge University Press, 1966), pp. 81–82.

35. Mao Tse-tung, op. cit., p. 5.

II. The Poems

沁園春 _{長沙 一九二五年}

獨立寒秋，湘江北去，橘子洲頭。看萬
山紅遍，層林盡染;漫江碧透，百舸爭
流。鷹擊長空，魚翔淺底，萬類霜天競
自由。悵寥廓，問蒼茫大地，誰主沉浮?
攜來百侶曾游。憶往昔崢嶸歲月

Changsha

I stand alone in cold autumn.
The River Hsiang goes north
around the promontory of Orange Island.
I see the thousand mountains gone red
and rows of stained forests.
The great river is glassy jade
swarming with one hundred boats.
Eagles flash over clouds
and fish float near the clear bottom.
In the freezing air a million creatures compete
     for freedom.
In this immensity
I ask the huge greenblue earth,
who is master of nature?

I came here with many friends
and remember those fabled months and years
     of study.
We were young,
sharp as flower wind, ripe,
candid with a scholar's bright blade
     and unafraid.
We pointed our finger at China

稠。恰同學少年，風華正茂；書生意氣，揮斥方遒。指點江山，激揚文字，糞土當年萬戶侯。曾記否，到中流擊水，浪遏飛舟？

and praised or damned through the papers
    we wrote.
The warlords of the past were cowdung.

Do you remember
how in the middle of the river
we hit the water, splashed, and how our waves
    slowed down the swift junks?

1925

Notes on the Poems begin on page 114.

菩薩蠻　黃鶴樓　一九二七年春

茫茫九派流中國，沉沉一綫穿南北。

煙雨莽蒼蒼，龜蛇鎖大江。　黃鶴知

何去？剩有游人處。把酒酹滔滔，心潮

逐浪高！

Tower of the Yellow Crane

China is vague and immense where the nine rivers pour.
The horizon is a deep line threading north and south.
Blue haze and rain.
Hills like a snake or tortoise guard the river.

The yellow crane is gone.
    Where?
Now this tower and region are for the wanderer.
I drink wine to the bubbling water—the heroes
    are gone.
Like a tidal wave a wonder rises in my heart.

Spring 1927

西江月 井冈山 一九二八年秋

山下旌旗在望，山头鼓角相闻。敌军围困万千重，我自岿然不动。　早已森严壁垒，更加众志成城。黄洋界上炮声隆，报道敌军宵遁。

38

Chingkang Mountain

Low on the mountain our flags and banners
and on the peak an echo of bugles and drums.
Around us a thousand circles of enemy armies
    yet we are rock.

No one cracks through our forest of walls,
    through our fortress of wills joined
    as one.
From the front lines at Huangyang the big guns roar
saying the enemy army fled in the night.

                  Fall 1928

清平樂　蔣桂戰爭　一九二九年秋

風雲突變，軍閥重開戰。灑向人間都是怨，一枕黃梁再現。　紅旗躍過汀江，直下龍岩上杭。收拾金甌一片，分田分地真忙。

Warlords

Wind and clouds suddenly rip the sky
and warlords clash.
    War again.
Rancor rains down on men who dream of a Pillow
of Yellow Barley.

Yet our red banners leap over the calm Ting River
    on our way
to Shanghang and to Lungyen the dragon cliff.
The golden vase of China is shattered.
    We mend it,
happy as we give away its meadows.

                September or October 1929

采桑子 重陽 一九二九年十月

人生易老天難老，歲歲重陽。今又重陽，戰地黃花分外香。

一年一度秋風勁，不似春光。勝似春光，寥廓江天萬里霜。

Ninth Day of the Ninth Moon

It is not the firmament but man who grows old,
for the ninth day of the ninth moon
    comes each year each year.
Today at the double yang,
yellow flowers on the battlefield are deeply fragrant.

One day each autumn a wind batters the land.
It is not spring light
yet better than spring
for the sky and seas are an enormous frosty horizon
    under the dome.

October 11, 1929

如夢令　元旦　一九三零年一月

寧化清流歸化，路隘林深苔滑。今日向何方，直指武夷山下。山下山下，風展紅旗如畫。

New Year's Day

Where are we going?
The road is narrow. Deep in the forest
      the moss is slippery
as we leave Ninghua, Ching, and Kweihua behind.
We head for the foot of the tea slope
      of Wuyi.
Below the mountain below the mountain,
wind blows our red banners like a painting.

                                             1929

減字木蘭花 廣昌路上 一九三零年二月

漫天皆白，雪裏行軍情更迫。頭上高山，風捲紅旗過大關。　此行何去？贛江風雪迷漫處。命令昨頒，十萬工農下吉安。

46

On the Road to Chian

The whole icy sky is white
and we are marching in the snow. No green pine.
Mountains tower over us.
    As we climb the pass
the wind plays open our red banners.

Where are we going?
To the River Kan in the haze of windy snow.
We were told what to do.
One hundred thousand workers and peasants marching on
Chian,
    city of luck.

February 1930

蝶戀花 從汀州向長沙　一九三零年七月

六月天兵征腐惡，萬丈長纓要把鯤
鵬縛。贛水那邊紅一角，偏師借重黃
公略。　百萬工農齊踊躍，席捲江西
直搗湘和鄂。國際悲歌歌一曲，狂飆
爲我從天落。

Tingchow to Changsha

In June our soldiers of heaven fight against evil
    and rot.
They have a huge rope to tie up the whale
    or fabulous cockatrice.
On the far side of the Kan waters the ground turns red
under the strategy of Huang Kung-lueh.

A million workers and peasants leap up joyfully
    and roll up Kiangsi like a mat.
As we reach the rivers of Hunan and Hupei
we sing the Internationale. It pierces us
like a whirlwind from the sky.

July 1930

漁家傲 反第一次大『圍剿』 一九三一年春

萬木霜天紅爛漫，天兵怒氣沖霄漢。

霧滿龍岡千嶂暗，齊聲喚，前頭捉了

張輝瓚。 二十萬軍重入贛，風煙滾

滾來天半。喚起工農千百萬同心幹，

不周山下紅旗亂。

關於共工頭觸不周山的故事：『淮
南子・天文訓』：『昔者共工與顓

50

First Siege

The forests are a red blooming in the frost sky.
The anger of our good soldiers climbs through the clouds.
Haze hangs over the Brook of Dragons and a thousand hills
    are dark.
We all cry out:
The general Chang Hui-tsan is taken at the front!

Our huge army pours into Kiangsi.
Wind and smoke whirl whirl through half the world.
We woke a million workers and peasants
to have one heart.
Below the mountain of Puchow an anarchy of red flags.

January or Spring 1931

漁家傲

白雲山頭雲欲立，白雲山下呼聲急，枯木朽株齊努力。槍林逼，飛將軍自重霄入。

七百里驅十五日，贛水蒼茫閩山碧，橫掃千軍如捲席。有人泣，爲營步步嗟何及！

52

Second Siege

Clouds pause over the Mountain of White Clouds,
yet below the Mountain of White Clouds
    is mad shouting,
and even hollow trees and dry branches conspire.
Our forest of rifles darts ahead
    like the ancient Flying General
    who flew out of heaven to chase Turki tribesmen
out of Mongolia.

In fifteen days a forced march of two hundred miles
through gray Kan waters and Min mountains of jade.
We sweep away their troops easily, like rolling up a mat.
Someone is crying,
sorry he moved his bastions slowly.

Summer 1931

菩薩蠻 大柏地 一九三三年夏

赤橙黃綠青藍紫，誰持彩練當空舞？
雨後復斜陽，關山陣陣蒼。　當年鏖
戰急，彈洞前村壁。裝點此關山，今朝
更好看。

Region of the Great Pines

Red orange yellow green blue violet.
Who is dancing in the sky—holding the colorful ribbon
    of the rainbow?
After rain the sun slanting down.
Undulating blue hills and passes.

That year the battle was hot at its peak.
Bullet holes pit all the front village walls.
Today they are decorations
and the hills and passes are beautiful.

Summer 1933

清平樂 會昌　一九三四年夏

東方欲曉,莫道君行早。踏遍青山人未老,風景這邊獨好。　會昌城外高峰,顚連直接東溟。戰士指看南粵,更加鬱鬱葱葱。

56

Huichang

Dawn wakes in the east.
Don't say we are marching early.
Though we stomp over all these green hills
    we are not yet old,
and from here the land is a wonder.

Beyond the walls of bright Huichang
    the peaks
tumble all the way to the ocean in the east.
Our soldiers point and look eagerly
    south to Kwangtung,
onion green and sensual in the distance.

Summer 1934

憶秦娥 娄山關 一九三五年二月

西風烈，長空雁叫霜晨月。霜晨月，馬蹄聲碎，喇叭聲咽。

雄關漫道真如鐵，而今邁步從頭越。從頭越，蒼山如海，殘陽如血。

58

Loushan Pass

A hard west wind,
in the vast frozen air wild geese shriek to the morning
    moon,
frozen morning moon.
Horse hoofs shatter the air
and the bugle sobs.

The grim pass is like iron
yet today we will cross the summit in one step,
cross the summit.
Before us greenblue mountains are like the sea,
the dying sun like blood.

February 1935

十六字令三首 一九三四年到一九三五年

山，快馬加鞭未下鞍。驚回首，離天三尺三。

其二

山，倒海翻江捲巨瀾。奔騰急，萬馬戰猶酣。

60

Three Songs

1

Mountain.
I whip my quick horse and don't dismount
and look back in wonder.
The sky is three feet away.

2

Mountain.
The sea collapses and the river boils.
Innumerable horses race
insanely into the peak of battle.

其三

山，刺破青天鍔未殘。天欲墮，賴以拄其間。

3

Mountain.
Peaks pierce the green sky, unblunted.
The sky would fall
but for the columns of mountains.

1934-35

七律 長征 一九三五年十月

紅軍不怕遠征難，萬水千山只等閒。
五嶺逶迤騰細浪，烏蒙磅礴走泥丸。
金沙水拍雲崖暖，大渡橋橫鐵索寒。
更喜岷山千里雪，三軍過後盡開顏。

The Long March

The Red Army is not afraid of hardship on the march,
    the long march.
Ten thousand waters and a thousand mountains are nothing.
The Five Sierras meander like small waves,
the summits of Wumeng pour on the plain like balls
    of clay.
Cliffs under clouds are warm and washed below by the River
    Gold Sand.
Iron chains are cold, reaching over the Tatu River.
The far snows of Minshan only make us happy
and when the army pushes through, we all laugh.

October 1935

念奴嬌　崑崙　一九三五年十月

横空出世，莽崑崙，閱盡人間春色。飛起玉龍三百萬，攪得周天寒徹。夏日消溶，江河橫溢，人或爲魚鼈。千秋功罪，誰人曾與評說？

前人所謂『戰罷玉龍三百萬，敗鱗殘甲滿天飛』，說的是飛雲。這裏借用一句，說的是雪山。夏日登岷山遠望，羣山飛舞，一片皆白。老百姓說當年孫行者過此，都是火焰山，就是他借了芭蕉扇搧滅了火，所以變白了。

Kunlun Mountain

Over the earth
the greenblue monster Kunlun who has seen
all spring color and passion of men.
Three million dragons of white jade
    soar
and freeze the whole sky with snow.
When a summer sun heats the globe
rivers flood
and men turn into fish and turtles.
Who can judge
a thousand years of accomplishments or failures?

而今我謂崑崙:不要這高,不要這多雪。安得倚天抽寶劍,把汝裁爲三截?一截遺歐,一截贈美,一截還東國。太平世界,環球同此涼熱。

Kunlun,
you don't need all that height or snow.
If I could lean on heaven, grab my sword,
    and cut you in three parts,
I would send one to Europe, one to America,
    and keep one part here
    in China
that the world have peace
and the globe share the same heat and ice.

October 1935

清平樂 六盤山 一九三五年十月

天高雲淡，望斷南飛雁。不到長城非好漢，屈指行程二萬。　六盤山上高峰，紅旗漫捲西風。今日長纓在手，何時縛住蒼龍？

Liupan the Mountain of Six Circles

Dazzling sky to the far cirrus clouds.
I gaze at wild geese vanishing into the south.
If we cannot reach the Long Wall
    we are not true men.
On my fingers I count the twenty thousand li we have
    already marched.

On the summit of Liupan
the west wind lazily ripples our red banner.
Today we have the long rope in our hands.
When will we tie up the gray dragon of the seven
    stars?

October 1935

沁園春 雪 一九三六年二月

北國風光，千里冰封，萬里雪飄。望長
城內外，惟餘莽莽；大河上下，頓失滔
滔。山舞銀蛇，原馳蠟象，原指高原，即
秦晉高原。 欲與
天公試比高。須晴日，看紅裝素裹，分
外妖嬈。 江山如此多嬌，引無數英

Snow

The scene is the north lands.
Thousands of li sealed in ice,
ten thousand li in blowing snow.
From the Long Wall I gaze inside and beyond
and see only vast tundra.
Up and down the Yellow River
the gurgling water is frozen.
Mountains dance like silver snakes,
hills gallop like wax bright elephants
trying to climb over the sky.
On days of sunlight
the planet teases us in her white dress and
       rouge.

雄競折腰。惜秦皇漢武,略輸文采;唐宗宋祖,稍遜風騷。一代天驕,成吉思汗,只識彎弓射大雕。俱往矣,數風流人物,還看今朝。

Rivers and mountains are beautiful
and made heroes bow and compete to catch the girl—
    lovely earth.
Yet the emperors Shih Huang and Wu Ti
were barely able to write.
The first emperors of the Tang and Sung dynasties
    were crude.
Genghis Khan, man of his epoch
and favored by heaven,
knew only how to hunt the great eagle.
They are all gone.

Only today are we men of feeling.

                    February 1936 or August 1945

七律 人民解放軍佔領南京 一九四九年四月

鍾山風雨起蒼黃,百萬雄師過大江。

虎踞龍盤今勝昔,天翻地覆慨而慷。

宜將剩勇追窮寇,不可沽名學霸王。

天若有情天亦老,人間正道是滄桑。

Capture of Nanking

Rain and a windstorm rage blue and yellow over Chung
    the bell mountain
as a million peerless troops cross the Great River.
The peak is a coiled dragon, the city a crouching tiger
    more dazzling than before.
The sky is spinning and the earth upside down.
    We are elated
yet we must use our courage to chase the hopeless enemy.
We must not stoop to fame like the overlord Hsiang Yu.
If heaven has feeling it will grow old
    and watch
our seas turn into mulberry fields.

April 1949

七律 和柳亞子先生 一九四九年夏

飲茶粵海未能忘,索句渝州葉正黃。
三十一年還舊國,落花時節讀華章。
牢騷太盛防腸斷,風物長宜放眼量。
莫道昆明池水淺,觀魚勝過富春江。

Poem for Liu Ya-tzu

I cannot forget how in Canton we drank tea
and in Chungking went over our poems
    when leaves were yellowing.
Thirty-one years ago and now we come back
    at last to the ancient capital
    Peking.
In this season of falling flowers I read
    your beautiful poems.
Be careful not to be torn inside.
Open your vision to the world.
Don't say that waters of Kumming Lake are too shallow.
We can watch fish better here than in the Fuchun
    River in the south.

                         Summer 1949

浣溪沙 和柳亞子先生　一九五零年十月

一九五零年國慶觀劇,柳亞子先生卽席賦浣溪沙因步其韻奉和。

長夜難明赤縣天,百年魔怪舞翩躚,人民五億不團圓。　一唱雄鷄天下白,萬方樂奏有于闐,詩人興會更無前。

Poem for Liu Ya-tzu

Night is long. And slowly comes the crimson sun-moon
    dawn.
Demons and monsters danced about and whirled
    for hundreds of years
and five hundred millions were not a family.

Yet in one song the cock whitens the world.
Song pours on us from ten thousand corners
and musicians from Khotan play. Never before
    were we poets so moved.

October 1950

浪淘沙 北戴河 一九五四年夏

大雨落幽燕，白浪滔天，秦皇島外打魚船。一片汪洋都不見，知向誰邊？

往事越千年，魏武揮鞭，東臨碣石有遺篇。蕭瑟秋風今又是，換了人間。

82

Peitaho

Heavy rains fall on Yuyen, the northland kingdom
 of swallows.
White pages of rain envelop the sky,
and fishing boats off the Island of the Emperor Chin
disappear on the ocean.
Which way have they gone?

More than a thousand years ago
the mighty emperor Tsao Tsao cracked his whip and drove
 his army against the Tartars.
He left us a poem: "Let us move east to the Stone
 Mountains."
Today we still shiver in the autumn gale,
 in desolate winds,
yet another man is in the world.

        Summer 1954

83

水調歌頭 游泳 一九五六年六月

纔飲長沙水，又食武昌魚。萬里長江橫渡，極目楚天舒。不管風吹浪打勝似閒庭信步，今日得寬餘。子在川上曰：逝者如斯夫！　風檣動，龜蛇靜起宏圖。一橋飛架，南北天塹變通途。更

Swimming

After swallowing some water at Changsha
I taste a Wuchang fish in the surf
and swim across the Yangtze River that winds
    ten thousand li.
I see the entire Chu sky.
Wind batters me, waves hit me—I don't care.
Better than walking lazily in the patio.
Today I have a lot of time.
Here on the river the Master said:
"Dying—going into the past—is like a river flowing."

立西江石壁，截斷巫山雲雨，高峽出
平湖。神女應無恙，當驚世界殊。

Winds flap the sail,
tortoise and snake are silent,
a great plan looms.
A bridge will fly over this moat dug by heaven
and be a road from north to south.
We will make a stone wall against the upper river
        to the west
and hold back steamy clouds and rain of Wu peaks.
Over tall chasms will be a calm lake,
and if the goddess of these mountains is not dead
she will marvel at the changed world.

June 1956

蝶戀花 答李淑一 一九五七年五月十一日

我失驕楊君失柳，楊柳輕颺直上重霄九。問訊吳剛何所有，吳剛捧出桂花酒。

寂寞嫦娥舒廣袖，萬里長空且爲忠魂舞。忽報人間曾伏虎，淚飛頓作傾盆雨。

88

The Gods

on the death of his wife
Yang Kai-hui

I lost my proud poplar and you your willow.
As poplar and willow they soar straight up
    into the ninth heaven
and ask the prisoner of the moon, Wu Kang, what is there.
He offers them wine from the cassia tree.

The lonely lady on the moon, Chang O,
    spreads her vast sleeves
and dances for these good souls in the unending sky.
Down on earth a sudden report of the tiger's defeat.
Tears fly down from a great upturned bowl of rain.

May 11, 1957

七律二首 送瘟神 一九五八年七月一日

讀六月三十日人民日報，餘江縣消滅了血吸蟲。浮想聯翩，夜不能寐。微風拂煦，旭日臨窗。遙望南天，欣然命筆。

綠水青山枉自多，華佗無奈小蟲何！

千村薜荔人遺矢，萬戶蕭疏鬼唱歌。

坐地日行八萬里，巡天遙看一千河。

牛郎欲問瘟神事，一樣悲歡逐逝波。

90

Saying Good-bye to the God of Disease (1)

Mauve waters and green mountains are nothing
when the great ancient doctor Hua To could not defeat
    a tiny worm.
A thousand villages collapsed, were choked with weeds,
    men were lost arrows.
Ghosts sang in the doorway of a few desolate houses.
Yet now in a day we leap around the earth
or explore a thousand Milky Ways.
And if the cowherd who lives on a star
    asks about the god of plagues,
tell him, happy or sad, the god is gone,
    washed away in the waters.

July 1, 1958

春風楊柳萬千條，六億神州盡舜堯。

紅雨隨心翻作浪，青山着意化爲橋。

天連五嶺銀鋤落，地動三河鐵臂搖。

借問瘟君欲何往，紙船明燭照天燒。

Saying Good-bye to the God of Disease (2)

Thousands of willow branches in a spring wind.
Six hundred million of China, land of the gods,
    and exemplary like the emperors Shun and Yao.
A scarlet rain of peach blossoms turned into waves
    and emerald mountains into bridges.
Summits touch the sky.
We dig with silver shovels
and iron arms shake the earth and the Three Rivers.
God of plagues, where are you going?
We burn paper boats and bright candles to light his way
    to heaven.

July 1, 1958

七律

一九五九年六月二十五日到韶山。離別這個地方已有三十二周年了。

别夢依稀咒逝川，故園三十二年前。

紅旗捲起農奴戟，黑手高懸霸主鞭。

爲有犧牲多壯志，敢教日月換新天。

喜看稻菽千重浪，遍地英雄下夕煙。

Return to Shaoshan

I regret the passing, the dying, of the vague dream:
my native orchards thirty-two years ago.
Yet red banners roused the serfs, who seized three-pronged
  lances
when the warlords raised whips in their black hands.
We were brave and sacrifice was easy
and we asked the sun, the moon, to alter the sky.
Now I see a thousand waves of beans and rice
    and am happy.
In the evening haze heroes are coming home.

                                        June 25, 1959

七律　登廬山　一九五九年七月一日

一山飛峙大江邊,躍上葱蘢四百旋。

冷眼向洋看世界,熱風吹雨灑江天。

雲橫九派浮黃鶴,浪下三吳起白煙。

陶令不知何處去,桃花源裏可耕田?

Climbing Lushan

The mountain looms firmly over the Great River.
I climb four hundred bends to its green lush peak.
With cool eyes I stare at the rim of mankind
    and the sea beyond.
Hot wind blows rain in the sky and down
    to the river.
Clouds over the nine tributaries and the floating yellow
    crane,
where waves ripple toward the Three Wu. White mist
    flies up.
Who knows where Tao, the ancient poet, has gone?
Is he farming in the Land of the Peach Blossoms?

July 1, 1959

七絕　爲女民兵題照　一九六一年二月

颯爽英姿五尺槍，曙光初照演兵場。

中華兒女多奇志，不愛紅裝愛武裝。

Militia Women

Early rays of sun illumine the parade grounds
and these handsome girls heroic in the wind,
    with rifles five feet long.
Daughters of China with a marvelous will,
you prefer hardy uniforms to colorful silk.

February 1961

七律 答友人 一九六一年

九嶷山上白雲飛,帝子乘風下翠微。

斑竹一枝千滴淚,紅霞萬朵百重衣。

洞庭波湧連天雪,長島人歌動地詩。

我欲因之夢寥廓,芙蓉國裏盡朝暉。

To a Friend

White clouds hang over the Mountain of Nine Questions.
The daughters of the emperor rode the wind
    down to a jade meadow
where a thousand tears fell and dappled the bamboo.
Now their dresses are a hundred folds of silk,
    a million sunclouds of red blossoms.

In Tungting Lake snow waves rise to heaven
and people of the Orange Island sing and make the earth
    vibrate.
I want to dream of the immense
land of the hibiscus shiny with young morning sun.

1961

七絕

爲李進同志題所攝廬山仙人洞照　一九六一年

九月九日

暮色蒼茫看勁松，亂雲飛渡仍從容。

天生一個仙人洞，無限風光在險峯。

Written on a Photograph of the
Cave of the Gods

At bluegreen twilight I see the rough pines
serene under the rioting clouds.
The cave of the gods was born in heaven,
a vast wind-ray beauty on the dangerous peak.

September 9, 1961

七律 和郭沫若同志　一九六一年十一月十七日

一從大地起風雷，便有精生白骨堆。

僧是愚氓猶可訓，妖為鬼蜮必成災。

金猴奮起千鈞棒，玉宇澄清萬里埃。

今日歡呼孫大聖，只緣妖霧又重來。

To Kuo Mo-jo

Wind. Lightning. Thunder over the earth
and a demon is born from a heap of white bones.
Slow Tripitaka can still be taught
yet the blind monster-insect—a horn in its mouth—
 spits and kills.
The gold monkey swings his mammoth club
and knocks ten thousand li of dust out of the air:
 the sky is transparent jade.
Today we cheer the Great Sage
for the demon mist rises again.

November 17, 1961

卜算子 詠梅 一九六二年十二月

讀陸游詠梅詞，
反其意而用之。

風雨送春歸，飛雪迎春到。已是懸崖百丈冰，猶有花枝俏。　俏也不爭春，只把春來報。待到山花爛熳時，她在叢中笑。

106

In Praise of the Winter Plum Blossom

Spring disappears with rain and winds
and comes with flying snow.
Ice hangs on a thousand feet of cliff
yet at the tip of the topmost branch the plum
      blooms.

The plum is not a delicious girl showing off
yet she heralds spring.
When mountain flowers are in wild bloom
she giggles in all the color.

December 1962

七律 冬雲 一九六二年十二月二十六日

雪壓冬雲白絮飛,萬花紛謝一時稀。

高天滾滾寒流急,大地微微暖氣吹。

獨有英雄驅虎豹,更無豪傑怕熊羆。

梅花歡喜漫天雪,凍死蒼蠅未足奇。

Winter Clouds

Winter clouds. Cotton snow falls heavily
like many disappearing flowers.
Icy brooks bubble high in the air
and on earth a slender wind is warm.
And the hero? He dominates the tiger
    and the leopard.
The wild bear cannot frighten a brave man.

Even the plum tree is pleased with snow
and doesn't care about freezing or dying
    houseflies.

December 26, 1962

滿江紅

和郭沫若同志　一九六三年一月九日

小小寰球，有幾個蒼蠅碰壁。嗡嗡叫，幾聲淒厲，幾聲抽泣。螞蟻緣槐誇大國，蚍蜉撼樹談何易。正西風落葉下長安，飛鳴鏑。

多少事，從來急；天地轉，光陰迫。一萬年太久，只爭朝夕。四

110

To Kuo Mo-jo

On our small planet
a few houseflies bang on the walls.
They buzz, moan, moon,
and ants climb the locust tree and brag about
      their vast dominion.
It is easy for a flea to say
it topples a huge tree.
In Changan leaves spill in the west wind,
the arrowhead groans in the air.

海翻騰雲水怒，五洲震盪風雷激。要

掃除一切害人蟲，全無敵。

We had much to do
and quickly.
The sky-earth spins
and time is short.
Ten thousand years is long
and so a morning and an evening count.
The four oceans boil and clouds fume with rain.
The five continents shake in the wind of lightning.
We wash away insects
and are strong.

January 9, 1963

NOTES ON THE POEMS

These notes are largely informational rather than interpretive. Although the poems are self-contained and do not depend on explanation to convey image, thought, and experience, it is useful to have some knowledge of mythological and historical allusions. Mao adds an author's note to a number of poems, giving mythological or historical references. The dating of the poems is in most cases certain. The emphasis in the summary of Chinese Versification (page 142) is on the forms used by Mao, which are also the main traditional forms in Chinese poetry.

W.B.

Changsha

TITLE   Changsha is the capital of Hunan, Mao Tse-tung's native province. The city is on the east bank of the Hsiang River, which flows north into the Yangtze. Mao studied in Changsha at the First Normal School of Hunan from 1913 to 1918.

Orange Island   Orange Island is in the Hsiang River, west of Changsha. Mao often went to the island with school friends or swam in waters nearby.

fabled   Also "turbulent" and "exciting."

papers we wrote   In September 1915 Yuan Shih-kai wanted to become emperor of China. Tang Hsiang-ming, the warlord then controlling Hunan, supported Yuan and banned all opposition to him. Nevertheless, Mao published a pamphlet opposing the restoration of monarchy.

FORM   After the *tzu Chin Yuan Chun,* meaning "Spring in the Garden of Chin." As indicated in the notes on Chinese Versification (page 142), the original *tzu* was a song or melody; here it concerns Chin Shui, a daughter of Emperor Ming of the West Han period. But as is often the case, the original is lost and also the melody. What remains is the pattern or form: the number of lines, the number of characters per line, the rhyme scheme, and the arrangement of tones. The poet has *filled in* the pattern. The subject matter need have, and in this case has, nothing to do with the original poem. Mao uses the same *tzu* for his poem "Snow."

Tower of the Yellow Crane

TITLE   The Tower of the Yellow Crane is a high tower on a cliff west of Wuchang in the province of Hupeh. There is a legend that the saint Tzu-an once rode past the area on a yellow crane, thought to be an immortal bird. Another legend holds that Fei Wen-wei attained immortality immediately at this spot and regularly flew past on a yellow or golden crane. To commemorate these events a tower was erected and the place became a pilgrimage site for scholars and poets.

nine rivers   The many tributaries of the Yangtze which flow nearby.

deep line threading north and south   Reference is probably to the Peking-Hankow railway, which links north and south.

snake or tortoise guard the river   Literally, snake or tortoise *grip* the river. The allusion is to Snake Hill and Tortoise Hill, which face each other on either bank of the Yangtze at Hankow.

I drink wine to the bubbling water   The Sung dynasty poet Su Tung-po wrote a poem in which he drank to the moon's reflection in the river while recalling old heroes. The implication is that like the yellow crane, the old heroes are gone.

FORM   After the *tzu Pu Sa Man,* meaning "Strange Goddess," composed in the Tang dynasty when a delegation from a kingdom of Amazons came to the Chinese court to pay tribute. These women

115

were known as the *Pu Sa Man*. They wore gold headgear in their tall coiffures and had many strings of pearls around their necks.

Chingkang Mountain

TITLE   An immense mountain in the Lo Hsiao range between Kiangsi and eastern Hunan provinces. In September 1927 Mao Tse-tung led the Red Army here and established his first revolutionary base. He was joined in April 1928 by his principal general, Chu Teh.

a thousand circles of enemy armies   Kuomintang troops attacked this base repeatedly in 1927 and 1928. The KMT Army was several times larger than the Red Army.

Huangyang   Mao's troops blocked all ways to the base except through the district of Huangyang, left open on purpose. There they ambushed the enemy and broke its offensive.

FORM   After the *tzu Hsi Chiang Yueh,* meaning "West River Moon." The phrase is from lines of Li Po (701–62): "Now the moon is still over the West River."

Warlords

TITLE   The full title is "War between Chiang and the Kwangsi Group." While Chiang Kai-shek was fighting with other military leaders of Kwangsi, Mao and Chu Teh accomplished their plan of setting up a base in north Fukien province. In the same area the Red Army took Shanghang at dawn on September 21, 1929. Lungyen—Dragon Cliff—was taken earlier in the year.

Pillow of Yellow Barley   Yellow Barley or Golden Millet. There is a Tang dynasty story of a poor scholar, Lu Sheng, who meets an immortal, Lu Weng, in an inn in Hantan. Lu Sheng complains of his harsh life and the god lends him a pillow, a pillow on which he can sleep and dream of good fortune. He sleeps and all his ambitions appear to come true: honor, wealth, power, marriage to a beautiful girl, and old age. When he wakes up, the innkeeper, a Taoist friend,

116

is cooking a meal for him of golden millet. But it is not yet cooked.
The Pillow of Yellow Barley suggests the ambitious dreams of men.

Ting River   Ting means "flat" or "calm."

golden vase of China   Mao compares China to a golden vase
fragmented by the warlords. He mends the vase—that is, he reunites
the land—then he gives its meadows away. He is speaking of land
reform and land redistribution.

FORM   After the *tzu Ching Ping Lo,* meaning "Pure Joy"; perhaps
from a poem by Li Po.

Ninth Day of the Ninth Moon

TITLE   The ninth day of the ninth moon, by the lunar calendar, is a
holiday. On this day the sun and moon are yang—that is, in their
male or maximum position. It is a day of celebration, of feasting. It is
customary to go up a hill to avoid epidemics, and to visit the graves
of ancestors. The ninth day of the ninth moon, or double ninth day,
occurred October 11, 1929, after a successful campaign in western
Fukien.

FORM   After the *tzu Tsai Sang Tzu,* meaning "Song of Picking
Mulberries."

New Year's Day

TITLE   The poem was written on New Year's Day by the Western
solar, not the Chinese lunar, calendar.

Ninghua, Ching, and Kweihua   In 1929 Mao and General Chu
Teh led the Red Army eastward from Chingkang Mountain to open
up new revolutionary bases in western Fukien and southern Kiangsi
provinces. Ninghua, Ching, and Kweihua are names of counties in
Fukien province.

Wuyi   As Mount Hymettus in Greece is famous for its honey, so
Wuyi Mountain in China is famous for its tea.

FORM   After the *tzu Ju Meng Ling,* meaning "Like a Dream." The original *tzu* was by the Tang emperor Chuang Tsung, who reigned from 923 to 926.

On the Road to Chian

TITLE   The Red Army attacked Chian at least nine times in 1930. This poem records the first, an attack in the snow in February of that year. Chian is in the middle of Kiangsi province. The original title is "On the Road to Kwangchang." Kwangchang lies beyond Chian.

line 2   In a later edition this line was changed. The new line might be translated as "Marching in the snow made our situation more urgent."

Mountains tower over us   Reference is to the Yunshan range.

River Kan   The Kan is the main river of Kiangsi province. It flows into Lake Poyang and then into the Yangtze.

FORM   After the *tzu Mu Lan Hua,* meaning "The Magnolia." It was composed, as an abbreviated song, by the Southern Tang emperor Li Yu, who reigned from 962 to 975.

Tingchow to Changsha

TITLE   Mao and the army are on their way to attempt to capture Nanchang. The attack, as well as one soon after on Changsha, failed.

soldiers of heaven   It is suggested that the soldiers are carrying out the will of heaven.

huge rope   In the Han dynasty (206 B.C.–220 A.D.) General Chung Chun asked the emperor Wu Ti for a long cord, with which he pledged to bind and bring back as captive the king of southern Yueh, who led the invading troops. See note on *long rope* in "Liupan the Mountain of Six Circles," page 125. Here the reference is obviously to the KMT armies, not the Japanese.

whale or fabulous cockatrice   The reference is to a big fish, a whale, that turns into a roc or cockatrice. Chuang-tzu (c. 275 B.C.)

118

described a whale in the north sea that turned into a giant roc floating on a whirlwind. Jorge Luis Borges in the *Book of Imaginary Beings* describes the roc (also given as "rukh") as "a vast magnification of the eagle or vulture." He says: "Marco Polo adds that some envoys from China brought the feather of a *Rukh* back to the Grand Khan. A Persian illustration in Lane shows the Rukh bearing off three elephants in its beak and talons. . . ."

Huang Kung-lueh   The commander in charge of the right flank in this operation. In 1931, a year later, he was killed in action at Chian.

Hunan and Hupei   Operations were carried out in these two provinces in July of the same year.

FORM   After the Tang *tzu Tieh Lien Hua,* meaning "Butterflies Courting Flowers."

First Siege

TITLE   The full title is "Opposing the First Siege." In the Introduction the First Siege is referred to as the First Annihilation Campaign. It is also called the First Encirclement. See Introduction for background material.

Brook of Dragons   In Chinese, Lung Kang, a place name where the five-day battle of the First Siege began December 27, 1930.

The general Chang Hui-tsan   Chang Hui-tsan was a Hunan warlord who directed front-line operations at the battle of Lung Kang. The field commander was captured.

Mao has an extensive commentary on the last line, giving three versions of the Chinese myth to which he is referring. The note concerns three stories about a hero, Kung Kung; then Mao adds his own rendering. All four versions are fascinating, although it is not clear how they relate to the last line of the poem. Mao writes: "The three accounts vary and I prefer the *Huai Nan Tzu* by Liu An (178–122 B.C.) in which Kung Kung was a victorious hero. Liu An writes: 'Kung Kung was angry and knocked his head against the mountain of Puchow, breaking the pillar that supported heaven and

119

held up the earth. After this the sky leaned toward the northwest, and the sun, moon, stars and constellations also moved in that direction. The earth then became lower, and waters, floods, dust and mud flowed southeast toward the earth.' Did Kung Kung die or not? There is no clear account but it appears that he actually won.''

FORM   After the *tzu Yu Chia Ao,* meaning "Fishermen's Pride.'' The original *tzu* was by Yen Shu (991–1040).

Second Siege

TITLE   The full title is "Opposing the Second Siege.'' See Introduction for background material on the Annihilation Campaigns.

Mountain of White Clouds   Some eighty li east of Huichang county in Kiangsi province. (One li is approximately one-third of a mile.)

and even hollow trees and dry branches conspire   In the *People's Daily,* June 8, 1962, Kuo Mo-jo says that the hollow trees and dry branches refer to the enemy troops.

like the ancient Flying General   The text does not include "to chase Turki tribesmen/out of Mongolia,'' although without this explanation the previous line is quite meaningless to a Western reader. Reference is to the well-known Han general Li Kuang, who defended the kingdom against Turki tribes then occupying Mongolia. Because of his swift movements he became known as the Flying General.

We sweep away their troops   From a line by Tu Fu (712–70): "My pen alone sweeps away a thousand strong men.''

like rolling up a mat   From a line in "On the Mistakes of Chin Shih Huang'' by Chia Yi (201–169 B.C.).

Someone is crying   Chiang Kai-shek. Chiang is regretting his strategy of slow advance, of placing a bastion at every step.

FORM   After the *tzu Yu Chia Ao,* meaning "Fishermen's Pride.'' Same form in "First Siege.''

120

Region of the Great Pines

TITLE   Tapoti, meaning "Region of the Great Pines," is a district near Juichin county in Kiangsi province. A revolutionary base was established there which Chiang Kai-shek attacked four times between the end of 1930 and February 1933. He failed in each attempt.

FORM   After the *tzu Pu Sa Man,* meaning "Strange Goddess." See note on FORM in "Tower of the Yellow Crane," page 115.

Huichang

TITLE   In January 1929 Mao led the Red Army into Huichang county to establish the southern Kiangsi base. Huichang borders on Fukien province in the east and Kwangtung province in the south.

bright   The Chinese characters for Huichang are a compound or double character, the second of which is a small sun (a square with a horizontal line in the middle) over a bigger sun. This is the word for "bright." See Chinese title. To translate Huichang as one word alone would not convey the suggestiveness of the original.

onion green and sensual in the distance   These words are an allusion to a line in the biography of Emperor Kwang Wu in the *Annals of the Later Han Dynasty*. The character here for "green" also means "onion."

FORM   After the *tzu Ching Ping Lo,* meaning "Pure Joy"; perhaps from a poem by Li Po.

Loushan Pass

Poem written during the Long March

TITLE   The Loushan (Lou Mountain) Pass is in the north of Tsunyi county in Kweichow province. It was a strategic position between this province and Szechuan, commanding the difficult road from Kweichow and Szechuan. The pass dominates the highest peak of the

Loushan range. Around it are three swordlike peaks. The road winding up the mountain made it difficult to take. The Red Army took the pass twice in 1935. The occasion of this poem was the second storming of the pass.

FORM   After the *tzu Yi Chin,* meaning "Remembering the Beauty of Chin." Chin was a girl of the palace. The name of this *tzu* comes from a poem by Li Po.

Three Songs

TITLE   Three songs of sixteen characters each, written in 1934 and 1935 during the Long March.

and look back in wonder   This phrase suggests a poem by Tu Fu, "Gazing at the Peaks," in which he looks back at the grandeur of Mount Tai.

The sky is three feet away   Mao adds a note to this poem, quoting a folk song:

> The Skull mountain is above,
> Treasure Mountain is below.
> The sky is only three feet away.
> If you cross on foot you must bend your head,
> if on a horse you must dismount.

FORM   After the *tzu Shih Liu Tzu Ling,* meaning "Song of Sixteen Characters."

The Long March

Poem written during the Long March.

TITLE   On October 16, 1934, the Red Army set out from its base in Kiangsi. It fought continuously through ten provinces, frequently doubling back on its tracks. The army often traveled by night in the epic 6,500-mile march. Its final destination was Shensi, where it established a new anti-Japanese base, but the army was forced to wander over much of China, reaching even to the borders of Tibet. A small percentage of the original army survived. It was, however, the decisive moral venture of the revolution and it established Mao Tse-tung as the undisputed leader of the movement. There are many descriptions of the Long March. See André Malraux's *Anti-Memoirs*, Robert Payne's *Portrait of a Revolutionary: Mao Tse-tung*, Jerome Ch'ên's *Mao and the Chinese Revolution*, and Edgar Snow's *Red Star over China*.

Five Sierras These ranges spread through four provinces: Hunan, Kwangtung, Kwangsi, and Kweichow. The five ranges are Tayu, Chitien, Tupang, Mengchu, and Yuecheng.

Wumeng A high mountain range between Kweichow and Yunnan provinces.

River Gold Sand A river in the upper reaches of the Yangtze in Yunnan province. A difficult crossing took place there.

Tatu River A tributary of the Yangtze at the Szechuan-Sikang border. Over the Tatu River was the Luting bridge, consisting of thirteen iron chains and some loose planks of wood. The bridge was heavily fortified and most of the planks had been removed. Twenty-four volunteers, crossing by hanging from the chains themselves, made a frontal assault and secured the other side. This crossing has been recounted in many books, has become the subject of plays and operas, and has passed into modern Chinese mythology. See Introduction.

Minshan A snow-covered mountain range in Chinghai, Kansu, Shensi, and Szechuan provinces. It was the last major obstacle of the March. Its highest crest was stormed September 14, 1935, with the aid of Miao tribe troops from Kweichow.

FORM A *lu shih,* an eight-line poem with seven characters in each line.

Kunlun Mountain

Poem written during the Long March.

NOTE ON POEM BY MAO TSE-TUNG "An ancient poet said, 'Three million dragons of white jade are fighting, their broken scales fly all

over the sky.' In this way he described the flying snow, but here I
have used it to describe snowy mountains. In summer, when one
climbs the Min Mountain, one looks out on far mountains that seem
to dance and shine in dazzling whiteness. There was a saying among
the people that years ago when the Monkey King (Sun Hsing-che)
passed by, all the mountains were of fire. But he borrowed a
palm-leaf fan and quenched the flame and that is why the mountains
froze and turned white."

Mao takes the image of the dragons of white jade from an
eleventh-century poet, Chang Yuan, of Huachow.

TITLE   Kunlun is a mountain on the upper reaches of the Khotan
River in Sinkiang province. The name is also used for the Karakoram
range, which runs from Tibet and Sinkiang into central China and
includes mountains such as the Minshan in Chinghai. The title can
also be translated simply "Kunlunshan"; *shan* means "mountain" or
"mountains" and is added to proper nouns; e.g., Minshan or Min
Mountain.

fish and turtles   In the first year of Chao Kung, praise for Yu's
flood-prevention work is recorded in a saying of Liu Ting-kung:
"Without Yu, we would have become fish." The Yangtze and Yellow
rivers both have their source in the Kunlun mountains, and in
summer, when the snow melts, these rivers flood.

FORM   After the *tzu Nien Nu Chiao,* meaning "The Girl Nien Nu."
Nien Nu was a famous palace singer of the eighth century.

Liupan the Mountain of Six Circles

Poem written during the Long March.

TITLE   Liupan is a high mountain southwest of Kuyuan county in
southern Kansu. It is so steep that the road to the summit circles
around six times. Toward the end of the Long March, in September
1935, the Red Army entered the area; the First Front Army under
Mao captured Liupan in October, and advanced into Shensi province.

Long Wall   The Great Wall of China in Chinese is the "Long
Wall." See Introduction.

long rope   In the Han dynasty (206 B.C.–220 A.D.) General Chung Chun asked the emperor Wu Ti for a long cord, with which he pledged to bind and bring back as captive the king of southern Yueh, who led the invading "barbarians." The reference may be to the Japanese, or to any enemy force.

gray dragon   The classical Chinese name for a constellation of seven stars in the eastern sky. According to the Peking edition of Mao's poems, *Nineteen Poems of Mao Tse-tung*, the dragon refers to the invading Japanese army, and these last lines may indicate a determination to go north to battle against the Japanese. In Robert Payne's biography of Mao, however, Mao is quoted as saying that he is not referring to Chiang or any one obstacle. "I meant all the evils— the Japanese, the Kuomintang, the terrible social system." Payne writes further (page 233): "Nor should the red flag be taken to mean only the Communist flag, for there is a deliberate confusion between the red flag and the red banner carried by the ancient Chinese generals. Mao delighted in such confusions in the same way that Tang dynasty poets would deliberately write poems about the border warfare of their time, while pretending to be writing about wars a thousand years earlier." We see the red banner in such classical poems as that by the Tang dynasty poet Tsen Tsan in which he describes winter preparations for an advance against the Huns: "And the wind fails to move our frozen red flag."

FORM   After the *tzu Ching Ping Lo,* meaning "Pure Joy"; perhaps from a poem by Li Po. The same *tzu* form is used in the poem "Huichang."

Snow

DATE   There is confusion about the dating of this poem. In at least two editions of Mao's poems, February 1936 is given as the date of composition; and Joachim Schickel supports that date in *Mao Tse-tung: 37 Gedichte* (Munich: DTV, 1967, p. 107). Jerome Ch'ên suggests that the poem was written sometime in the winter of 1944–45, before Mao's August 1945 meeting with Chiang Kai-shek to discuss peace and unity. In Robert Payne's biography Mao is quoted as saying that he wrote the poem in August 1945 while taking his first trip in a plane, between Yenan and Chungking, for his meeting with Chiang. In this case, the panorama of Chinese landscape, with dancing-serpent snow mountains and elephant hills, may be thought of as seen from the air. Payne claims that the poem was written in reply to another by Mao's friend Liu Ya-tzu (see two poems by Mao to Liu), and that he gave it to Liu August 28, 1945, at the Chungking airport. In the 1958 English-language edition of *Nineteen Poems*, the annotation states that Liu wrote a poem of his own in the same meter and Mao's poem is a reply. It is Mao's best-known poem.

In a recent edition of Mao's poems (*Annotations of Chairman Mao's Poetry*, Hong Kong: Kunlun Publishing Co., 1968, vol. 2) the editor, Chang Syang, returns to February 1936 as the date of composition: "The poem 'Snow' was written in February, four months after the victorious Long March, just after the Red Army arrived at its base in Yenan. On a certain day during a snowstorm, Chairman Mao went up a high mountain and took in the distant view. He saw the marvelous scene of a thousand li of flying snow over this whole territory."

Liu's son, Professor Liu Wu-chi of Indiana University, has offered the following information for this edition: "I was in Chungking with my father when Mao Tse-tung visited him at his temporary lodging in the campus of Nankai Middle School. I know that Mao showed my father the poem 'Snow' (probably Mao wrote 'Snow' first and my father's poem was a response), and later, in early September 1945, my father had the poem published in the *Hsin Hua* [*New China Daily*], the only Communist newspaper in Chungking. This was also the first time that one of Mao's poems appeared in a major publication. As for my father's meeting Mao at the airport or sending him off, I was not aware of this at the time."

mountains   Note by Mao Tse-tung: "These highlands are those of Shensi and Shansi provinces." Joachim Schickel notes that these provinces would not have been seen by Mao in a plane traveling from Yenan to Chungking and rejects 1945 as the year of composition in part for this reason.

Shih Huang   First emperor of the Chin dynasty, who ruled from 247/6 to 210 B.C. See Note 1 of Introduction.

Wu Ti   Emperor of the Han dynasty, who ruled from 140 to 87
B.C. The Chinese text carried the names of these emperors: Tai Tsung
of the Tang dynasty, who ruled from 627 to 649; Tai Tsu of the Sung
dynasty, who ruled from 960 to 976.

were barely able to write; crude   These epithets have been
translated in various ways to suggest, in a forceful way, the emperors'
lack of polish and literary talent.

Genghis Khan   The famous Mongol conqueror, who ruled from
1206 to 1227.

FORM   After the *tzu Chin Yuan Chun,* meaning "Spring in the
Garden of Chin." See note on FORM in "Changsha," page 114.

Capture of Nanking

TITLE   The full title of this poem is "The Capture of Nanking by the
People's Liberation Army (PLA)." Nanking had been the national
capital several times. It was at this time the capital of the Kuomintang
government.

Chung   Chung or Chungshan (Chung Mountain) lies east of
Nanking. Chung means "bell," hence "Chung the bell mountain."

Great River   The Yangtze.

The peak is a coiled dragon, the city a crouching tiger   Classical
writers referred to the city as a crouching tiger and the Chung
Mountain as a coiled dragon.

the overlord Hsiang Yu   In the third century B.C., during the Chin
dynasty, Hsiang Yu, also called Pa Wang, defeated a rival, Liu Pang.
Wishing to appear generous, however, he allowed Liu Pang to
occupy the western part of the empire. Eventually Liu Pang occupied
the whole country and defeated Hsiang Yu, who committed suicide.

If heaven has feeling   From a poem by the Tang poet Li Ho in
which it is said that heaven, upon seeing a parting, will grow old. In
the preface to the same poem, Li Ho writes that in the year 233, the
emperor Ming Huang gave orders to move some bronze statues of

the Buddha. When the statues were put in a cart they wept. Since the statues were inanimate yet were capable of weeping, so heaven, also inanimate, could have feeling and grow old. Heaven in the universe corresponds to authority. The Peking three-volume commentary on the poems suggests that the authority is the Kuomintang.

mulberry fields   According to an old Chinese myth, a certain woman lived to be so old that she repeatedly saw the seas dry up and turn into mulberry fields.

FORM   A *lu shih.*

Poem for Liu Ya-tzu (1949)

TITLE   Liu Ya-tzu was a well-known Chinese poet and statesman, and a close literary friend of Mao's.

Canton; Chungking   In the years 1925 and 1926 Mao Tse-tung was in Canton engaged in studies and lectures in connection with the agrarian movement. The two friends used to drink tea together. This part of the poem recalls the often translated poem by the Greek poet Kallimachos (b. 305 B.C.) on the death of his friend the poet Herakleitos. Both are works of recollection, and speak of poets speaking of poems. The reference to Chungking is to the year 1945, when Liu met Mao in the city. Mao had come to negotiate with Chiang Kai-shek. There in Chungking Mao gave Liu Ya-tzu the text of his poem "Snow," which it appears that he wrote in reply to a poem by Liu. See discussion in note on "Snow."

Thirty-one years ago   Mao first came to Peking in September 1918. See Introduction. The poem was written thirty-one years later, on his return in 1949.

season of falling flowers   Reference is to a line by Tu Fu (712–70): "At this season of falling flowers we meet again."

Kumming Lake   The lake at the Summer Palace in Peking.

Fuchun River   The Fuchun River goes through a province in the south. In the Later Han dynasty, the poet Yen Kuang preferred not to

128

live at court and he retired to the country, where he became a fisherman on the Fuchun River in the south. Mao is drawing a parallel with Liu Ya-tzu, who wished to retire to his native province. In attempting to persuade Liu Ya-tzu to stay in Peking and join the movement now that the revolution has been won, Mao uses the gentle argument that watching fish together in Peking is at least as good as observing them in the Fuchun River.

Poem for Liu Ya-tzu (1950)

MAO TSE-TUNG'S NOTE   "While we were watching performances during the national celebration of 1950 (the founding of the People's Republic on October 1, 1949), Mr. Liu Ya-tzu composed an impromptu poem after the *tzu Wan Hsi Sha* and I replied with another, filling in the same *tzu.*" (See Chinese Versification, page 142, for the *tzu.*) Mao composed his reply the next day, October 2, 1950.

TITLE   See preceding poem, also entitled "Poem for Liu Ya-tzu." The title in Chinese is "Reply to Liu Ya-tzu."

Night is long   The period before the revolution.

sun-moon dawn   This single character, one of several signifying brightness, contains the character for "sun" next to the character for "moon."

Khotan   In Han times this was the name of a country in Sinkiang in which the Uighur people lived. When Mao wrote the poem he was attending a performance that included Uighur dances.

FORM   After the *tzu Wan Hsi Sha*, meaning "Sands of the Wan Stream," a Tang dynasty song.

LIU YA-TZU'S POEM

Washing Stream Sand

In the evening of October 3, I went to the Hall of Cherished Virtue to watch the singing and dancing performance by joint troupes of the literary workers of the southwest ethnic groups, the Sinkiang, Kirin (Yen-pien), and Inner Mongolia groups. Chairman Mao asked me to compose a song to record the splendor of this grand occasion.

Trees on fire, flowers silver bright, night turned into day,
as brothers and sisters gracefully danced
their songs permeating the full moon.*

Were it not for this one man, our great leader,
how could one hundred races rejoice together?
A wonderful evening, this festival, no great joys known
    before.

Translated by Liu Wu-chi

Peitaho

TITLE   Peitaho means Peita River (*ho* is "river"). It is the name of a well-known summer resort town on the Yellow Sea, situated on the western shore of the Island of Emperor Chin (Chinwangtao) in Hopei province.

Yuyen   An old name for Hopei province. It means Northland Kingdom of Swallows; the *Yu* of Yuyen also refers to Yuchow, the *Yen* to the Kingdom of Yen.

Island of the Emperor Chin   See note on TITLE.

Emperor Tsao Tsao   General Tsao Tsao was the founder of the Kingdom of Wei in the Three Kingdoms period (220–80). He became known posthumously as Emperor Wu of Wei.

cracked his whip and drove his army against the Tartars   Tsao Tsao drove his army against the Wuhuan Tartars in 207 A.D. He passed Chiehshih, a rocky cliff near Peitaho. The cliff or promontory has since sunk into the sea.

---

*"The full moon" is the name of one of the folk songs, accompanied by dancing, sung by the Kazak ethnic groups from Sinkiang.

"Let us move east to the Stone Mountains"   Tsao Tsao left us a poem whose first line reads: "Let us move east to the Stone Mountains [Chiehshih]."

autumn gale   From the same poem by the Emperor Tsao Tsao.

FORM   After the *tzu Lang Tao Sha,* meaning "Sands Cleaned by Waves," from the later Tang dynasty.

Swimming

TITLE   In May 1956, at the age of sixty-two, Mao swam across the Yangtze River from Wuchang to Hankow. He swam the river two other times that summer, crossing the other way, back to Wuchang.

Changsha   City on the Hsiang River where Mao studied at the First Normal School of Hunan from 1913 to 1918. See note on poem "Changsha," page 114. The first two lines are an allusion to a folk song of the period of the Three Kingdoms (220–64): "We would rather drink the waters of Chienyeh [Nanking]/than taste the fish of Wuchang."

Chu sky   In the period of the Warring States (474–221 B.C.), Wuchang was in the Kingdom of Chu.

Master   Confucius (551–479 B.C.).

tortoise and snake   The allusion is to Snake Hill and Tortoise Hill, which face each other on either bank of the Yangtze at Hankow. There is a bridge between these two hills. On his second swim from Hankow to Wuchang, Mao entered the water under the arch of this bridge.

moat   The moat dug by heaven is the Yangtze, which in Kung Fan's biography, *Book of the South*, is described as nature's barrier between the north and south.

Wu peaks   Wu peaks or Wushan (*shan* is "mountain"). Wushan is a famous mountain in the Yangtze gorges.

calm lake   Lake of the reservoir.

goddess of these mountains   There is a legend that King Hsiang of Chu (294–264 B.C.) dreamed of a goddess of Wushan Mountain who controlled the clouds and rain (see fourth line from bottom). If she left in the morning, she brought steamy clouds; if in the evening, she brought rain.

The Gods

TITLE   Poem written for Li Shu-yi, a teacher in the Tenth Middle School at Changsha, the widow of Liu Chi-hsun. Liu was killed in the battle of Hunghu in Hupeh in September 1933. Mao sent the poem to the widow Li with the following note: "I am sending you a poem describing an imaginary journey to heaven. This is different from other ancient *tzus* in this style in that the author himself is not the traveler. . . ." Liu was secretary general of the Provincial Peasants Association and a friend of the poet.

The poem is addressed to Li and also to Mao's wife Yang Kai-hui, whom Mao had married in the winter of 1921. In 1930 the KMT general Ho Chien arrested Yang Kai-hui and Mao's sister Mao Tse-hung. General Ho insisted that Yang Kai-hui renounce her marriage to Mao. She refused and was beheaded. Mao Tse-hung was also executed. See Introduction for C. M. Bowra's commentary on the poem.

proud poplar and you your willow   Poplar refers to Mao's wife Yang, for the character for the name Yang also means "poplar." Willow refers to Liu Chi-hsun, for the character for the name Liu also means "willow." Thus for poplar and willow, we may substitute the names Yang and Liu. The character for "proud" also has an intended secondary meaning of "sensual" or "charming."

Wu Kang   According to an old legend Wu Kang committed some crimes while seeking immortality. His punishment was to go to the moon and cut down the cassia tree. The tree was five thousand feet in height and before each new blow of the ax it would grow whole again. Thus he had to go on felling it forever. It is a Sisyphean labor.

132

wine from the cassia tree   Wine made from the flowers of the cassia tree is wine of the gods or the immortals. In going to the moon Yang and Liu have become gods or immortals.

The lonely lady of the moon, Chang O   According to tradition the beautiful Chang O in the Hsia period (2205–1766 B.C.) stole the elixir of immortality from the Western Mother Goddess. She fled to the moon to become its goddess. But she is lonely in her realm. As the Tang poet Li Shang-yin (813–58) wrote: "Each night she longs for green seas and blue skies." However, she greets the new souls from the earth, Yang and Liu, and entertains them.

tiger's defeat   The tiger is probably Chiang Kai-shek.

tears   Tears of joy.

upturned bowl of rain   The characters usually translated as torrential or heavy rain mean literally an upturned bowl of rain. This meaning follows the Chinese image.

FORM   After the Sung *tzu Tien Lien Hua,* meaning "Butterflies Courting Flowers." The *tzu* is based, however, on an earlier Tang song, *Chiao Ta Chih,* meaning "Magpie Perching on a Branch." In reference to Mao's statement that in his poem he does not accompany the gods or immortals, he is referring to a kind of poem begun by Chu Yuan (340–278? B.C.), often called the father of Chinese poetry, who in his poem "Far Wanderings" accompanies the immortals.

Saying Good-bye to the God of Disease (1)

MAO TSE-TUNG'S NOTE   "After reading in the *People's Daily* of June 30, 1958, that in Yukiang county the parasitic leech the schistosome had been eliminated, my head was so filled with thoughts that I could not sleep. As a slight breeze came and blew in the dawn, and early morning sun came and knocked at the window, I looked at the distant southern skies and happily guided my pen into composing a poem."

133

TITLE   This poem and the one following are separate yet related poems, each on the subject of eliminating disease. Schistosomiasis, found also in Egypt and North Africa, had plagued many districts south of the Yangtze. A commission was set up in 1956 and in June 1958 it was reported that the parasites and the disease had been eradicated in Yukiang county in Kiangsi, as a result of filling in infected ponds, irrigation projects, and a new cure which shortened the disease's duration from months to a few days. The reference to southern skies is to the areas most troubled by the disease.

doctor Hua To   A great doctor of the Three Kingdoms period (220–64), equivalent to Asklepios and Hippokrates.

cowherd   Cowherd is the name of a constellation where the cowherd lives. Being from a farm, the cowherd has an interest in farmland problems, and so may ask about the problems of this disease.

FORM   A *lu shih.*

Saying Good-bye to the God of Disease (2)

Shun and Yao   Shun and Yao were model emperors, praised by Confucianists for their exemplary virtue. They are semilegendary figures. Yao is said to have reigned from 2286 to 2256 B.C. and Shun from 2256 to 2207 B.C.

scarlet rain   In a poem by the Tang poet Li Ho (790–876), peach blossoms shower down like scarlet rain.

the Three Rivers   Huangho, Huaiho, and the Loho; *ho* means "river."

We burn paper boats   After addressing the god of disease, Mao sends him ceremonially off into the next world.

FORM   A *lu shih.*

Return to Shaoshan

MAO TSE-TUNG'S NOTE   "On June 25, 1959, after an absence of 32 years."

134

TITLE   Shaoshan in Hunan province is Mao's native village. See Introduction. He had organized peasants in associations to work for better working conditions from the landlords. He was forced to flee in the summer of 1927. This poem marks his first return to the village.

FORM   A *lu shih*.

Climbing Lushan

TITLE   Lushan, or Lu Mountain, is a summer resort in Kiangsi province.

the Great River   The Yangtze River.

nine tributaries   Nine tributaries of the Yangtze.

yellow crane   See note on the TITLE in "Tower of the Yellow Crane," page 115.

Three Wu   The ancient state of Wu is today Kiangsi province.

Tao, the ancient poet   The poet Tao was a prefect or magistrate in Pengtse county in Kiangsi province. He gave up his post to become a hermit. He wrote an essay, *"Tao hua yuan chi" (Land of the Peach Blossoms)*, in which he described an idyllic world free from the troubles of the time.

FORM   A *lu shih*.

Militia Women

TITLE   There is a subtitle, "Inscription on a Photograph."

hardy uniforms to colorful silk   This poem is said to have influenced Chinese styles of dress.

FORM   A four-line *chueh chu* (half a *lu shih*).

To a Friend

Mountain of Nine Questions   Chiuyi Mountain. In Chinese mythology it was a mountain of nine summits, each one representing

135

a distinct question of quest or wonder. The saintly emperor Shun was buried there.

daughters of the emperor The daughters of the legendary emperor Yao married the saintly emperor Shun. When he died, his wives wept over his grave by a bamboo grove, speckling or dappling them with their tears. This species of spotted bamboo now grows in Hunan and Kiangsi provinces.

Tungting Lake A large lake in Hunan province.

Orange Island Orange Island (also called Long Island) lies in the Hsiang River, west of Changsha, capital of Hunan. See the poem "Changsha."

land of the hibiscus A poetic name for Hunan. The desire for return to the land of the hibiscus means to Mao's native province, Hunan.

FORM   A *lu shih.*

Written on a Photograph of the Cave of the Gods

TITLE   There is a subtitle, "Taken by Comrade Li Chin." The cave itself is a scenic place on Lushan Mountain, in Mao's province of Hunan.

FORM   A four-line *chueh chu,* with seven characters in each line.

To Kuo Mo-jo (1961)

TITLE   The full title is "Reply to Comrade Kuo Mo-jo." Kuo had written a poem dealing with the Monkey King and his fight with the skeleton spirit. The subject of his poem comes from Wu Cheng-en's classical book *Journey to the West* (translated by Arthur Waley as *Monkey*). The allusions in the poem may be taken as references to the Sino-Soviet conflict.

Tripitaka In *Monkey*, the monk Tripitaka was accompanied by the Monkey on his long journey to India to acquire Buddhist sutras, which he later translated into Chinese.

FORM   A *lu shih.*

136

In Praise of the Winter Plum Blossom

TITLE   Mao's poem is a reply to a poem by the Sung dynasty poet Lu Yu (1125–1210) on the same theme. It reverses the ending of Lu's poem, however, which speaks of peach blossoms that will signify fallen petals and dust, with only the fragrance left.

the plum blooms   The poem recalls Sappho's comparing a girl to an apple ripening at the tip of the topmost branch.

FORM   After the *tzu Pu Suan Tzu*, meaning "Fortune Telling."

Winter Clouds

TITLE   The poem was composed on Mao's sixty-ninth birthday. Again the animals, tiger, leopard, bear, appear to refer to the problems of the Sino-Soviet dispute. As in the previous poem, the plum tree is used as a traditional symbol of firmness and integrity.

FORM   A *lu shih.*

To Kuo Mo-jo (1963)

TITLE   The full title is "Reply to Kuo Mo-jo." The poem has distinctly different sounds from others by Mao, with more onomatopoeia. The idiom is more colloquial. The hovering presence of the Sino-Soviet dispute is the subject.

the arrowhead groans in the air   Some commentators have interpreted this line to mean that one autumn, with the groaning arrowhead, the signal was given to begin the Sino-Soviet dispute. The interpretation is uncertain.

FORM   After the *tzu Man Chiang Hung,* meaning "Fully Red River."

137

III. Appendixes

THE TRANSLATION

Because Chinese poetry depends very much on images, and images translate more readily and with less loss than other poetic devices, we have had a tradition of excellent Chinese poems in English, beginning with those of Arthur Waley. Ezra Pound's Cathay versions, and translations by Kenneth Rexroth, Robert Payne, Carolyn Kizer, and others, are effective poems in English. They read as poems.

The present versions may be called a close translation. My colleague Ko Ching-po and I have studied each character and then sought an English equivalent. Nothing has been omitted. In a few cases I have thought it necessary to add a word when the original suggested something recognizable to a Chinese but not to a Western reader. Each case of these multiple-meaning words, a common obstacle or opportunity in matters of translation, is indicated in the notes on the poems. These versions differ from other translations in that proper nouns, especially place names, are often translated rather than left in Chinese; at times they are given the Chinese name followed by the English meaning. The Chiuyi Mountain becomes the "Mountain of Nine Questions." This may be thought of as the equivalent of translating phrases like "the Badlands" or "the White House." "Les Terrains Maudits" or "la Maison Blanche" would be more meaningful to a French reader than "les Badlands" or "la White House." Chinese is particularly rich in evocative proper nouns.

CHINESE VERSIFICATION

Lines of verse in classical Chinese poetry have a fixed number of characters per line, the number varying according to the form. Since characters are monosyllabic, one character equals one syllable, a five-character line has five syllables, and a seven-character line seven syllables. Each syllable in classical Chinese has one of four tones: *ping* (level), *shang* (rising), *chu* (falling), or *ju* (entering). The form of a poem depends on the tonal pattern, the line length (number of characters), and the rhyme scheme. These forms, though numerous, are fixed, and while the original poem giving rise to the form has often been lost, the pattern remains. Following Chinese tradition, before each poem Mao cites the poem or poem pattern he has followed. In effect, the poet *fills in* a set pattern with his own words. Words, it should be noted, are not necessarily monosyllabic but frequently disyllabic and trisyllabic, that is, compounded of two or three characters. The line is determined by the number of characters, however, not the number of words. Thus a four-character line might contain four, three, two words, or conceivably only one complete compound word.

The main Chinese forms are the *lu shih* and *tzu.* The *lu* and *tzu,* as they were used in the Tang and Sung dynasties, are those favored by Mao. But all these forms develop from earlier verse structures found in collections and poets of the ancient Chou dynasty (1122–221 B.C.).

The first major collection of Chinese poetry is the *Classic of Poetry (Shih Ching)*, also called the *Book of Songs.* It contains 305 songs composed between 1000 and 700 B.C. It was edited, we believe, by Confucius (551–479 B.C.), who selected what would be preserved from the bulk of literature from the early Chou dynasty. These poems, translated by Pound as the *Confucian Odes*, are divided between folk *(feng)* and court *(ya)* poems, with forty temple hymns *(sung),* all written in the early *shih* pattern of four characters per line. Somewhat later we have *Chu Tzu,* a collection mainly by Chu Yuan (340?–278? B.C.), who is often called the father of Chinese poetry. Chu Yuan wrote in a freer form than the four-character *shih* of the Confucian canon. Finally, in the same Chou dynasty, we have the *fu,* a very free prose poem, which was used more widely in Han dynasty poetry (206 B.C.–220 A.D.).

Mao has taken his models mainly from later Tang (618–907) and Sung (960–1127) poets. His forms are the Sung *tzu,* of indeterminate length, the Tang five- or seven-character *lu* of eight lines, and the *chueh chu,* which is a four-line variation of the *lu.* The *lu* as used in late Tang poets, especially by Tu Fu, is a rigorously determined form. Its full name is *lu shih; lu* means "law" and the phrase means "regulated verse." The poem consists of eight lines, all of which must be either five-syllabic or seven-syllabic. The same rhyme is used throughout the poem. The five-syllable poem has end-rhyme in the second, fourth, sixth, and eighth lines; the seven-syllable poem has end-rhyme optionally in the first line, and then again in the second, fourth, sixth, and eighth lines. The middle four lines must form two pairs of antithetical couplets. Slight variations permit eight patterns for the *lu shih* poem. Close to the *lu shih* is the *chueh chu* ("truncated verse"), which is a four-line poem with five or seven characters in each line. It is the shortest poem in Chinese, and if the lines have only five characters each, the poem contains only twenty syllables. It is the most compressed Chinese verse form, and from it came the Japanese *haiku,* which is three syllables shorter.

The *tzu* form (long and short verse lines) has more than six hundred set tonal patterns, derived from popular melodies. Despite this diversity and its more lyrical nature, it is considered more

143

rigid than the *lu shih,* or certainly more rigorously complex. The *tzu* is usually divided into two stanzas, of lines varying from one to eleven syllables or characters. It is regulated by strict tonal patterns, line lengths, and rhyme schemes. Its lexicon admits more colloquial words and expressions and so, despite strict forms, it is also more flexible than the *lu shih.* Most of Mao's poems are *tzu* songs.

Some of Mao's poems are replies to the themes of earlier Chinese poems, as "In Praise of the Winter Plum Blossom," based on a poem by Lu Yu (1125–1210). Both poems are in turn modeled after the fixed pattern of an earlier *tzu.* A poem may also be a reply to a contemporary poem, as are Mao's poems to his friend Liu Ya-tzu or Kuo Mo-jo. Both these modern poems are based on classical models.

144

MAO'S CALLIGRAPHY

from the opening passages of *Liupan the Mountain of Six Circles*

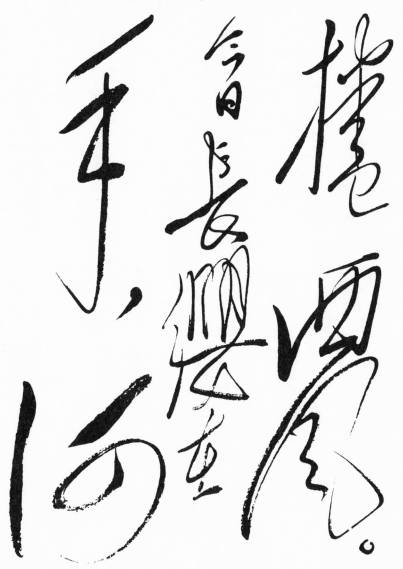

苍山如海，

红旗漫卷

残阳如血，

不到长城非好汉

天高雲淡，望斷南飛雁。

ABOUT THE TRANSLATORS

WILLIS BARNSTONE has supplied a great deal besides a good translation: his introduction, notes, short biography of Mao and history of the revolution, and notes on Chinese versification all combine to enrich the Western reader's understanding of Mao's poems. Barnstone's own book of poems, *From This White Island*, was nominated for a Pulitzer prize. His poems received the Cecil Hemley Memorial Award from the Poetry Society of America. As a scholar and editor, he has published a number of books on ancient and modern poetry, including many important translations. Mr. Barnstone is a graduate of Bowdoin, Columbia, Yale and the School of Oriental and African Studies at the University of London. He is currently Professor of Comparative Literature at Indiana University.

KO CHING-PO, who collaborated with Barnstone on the translations, is Professor of Comparative Literature at Indiana University. He was born in Mainland China and is a graduate of Williams College and Wesleyan University.

72 73 10 9 8 7 6 5 4 3 2 1